if you 're

clueless

about

insurance

and
want to
know more

by SETH GODIN

Dearborn
Financial Publishing, Inc.®

If You're Clueless about Insurance and Want to Know More

Editorial Director: Cynthia A. Zigmund
Managing Editor: Jack Kiburz
Interior and Cover Design: Karen Engelmann

© 1998 by Seth Godin Productions, Inc.

Published by Dearborn Financial Publishing, Inc.®

Printed in the United States of America

98 99 00 10 9 8 7 6 5 4 3 2 1

Library of Congress Cataloging-in-Publication Data
Godin, Seth.
    If you're clueless about insurance / Seth Godin
        p.   cm.
    Includes index.
    ISBN 0-7931-2718-1
    1. Insurance.   I. Title.
   HG8051.G57   1997
   368--dc21   97-26342
                                              CIP

Acknowledgments

Thanks to Jack Kiburz and Cindy Zigmund at Dearborn whose editorial guidance made this book possible. Karen Watts was the driving force behind the Clueless concept, and Lynn Adkins did an expert job of pulling it all together.

Thanks to Robin Dellabough, Lisa DiMona, Nana Sledzieski, Ann Weinerman, Emily Gold, Rachel Sussman, Susan Kushnick, Lisa Lindsay, Julie Maner, and Sarah Silbert at SGP for their never-ending insight and hard work. And kudos to Sidney Short for his layout work, Theresa Casaboon for her copyediting talent, and Suzanne Herel and Claire McKean for their expert proofreading.

Special thanks to Donna Hauser at Allstate Insurance and Roger T. Buchanan, Jr. of the Buchanan Agency for lending their expertise.

Contents

GETTING
a clue
about building
your insurance
PLAN

CHAPTER ONE
Purchasing insurance is paying money now to protect yourself from tomorrow's possibilities. It's about peace of mind and secure living, and it's easy to take control of, one step at a time—starting today!

Congratulations! By picking up this book, you've taken the first step toward a more secure future. And you couldn't have picked a better time. Because even if the thought of studying all that fine print on insurance policies makes your eyeballs cross—or if it occurs to you that knowing the ins and outs of your automobile liability coverage isn't going to make you the life of any party—the fact remains that you can't own a car without having it insured, and you can't buy a home without purchasing homeowner's insurance.

A really sound insurance strategy covers more than just your car or house. You may even have some health and disability insurance through your employer or through a private insurer. But as you grow and change, your insurance needs will, too. And although you don't have to plan for every insurance contingency all at once, you

should know what's available so you'll be ready to ask the right questions and make the appropriate decisions when it's necessary.

Insurance is all about managing downside risk. You buy insurance to protect yourself or your family members from unaffordable financial consequences that arise from unforeseeable events. The type and amount of insurance you buy is determined by weighing the financial repercussions of an occurrence against the likelihood that it will actually happen—and this book will show you how to do just that.

Most people don't spend a whole lot of time thinking about buying insurance. Maybe it's because it seems unsatisfying to spend money on something so intangible. Or because talking about life insurance brings you nose to nose with your own mortality. And many people don't even bother with flood or earthquake insurance because they think those kinds of disasters will never happen to them.

But you're smarter than that. You may be clueless now, but you have the street smarts to understand how important insurance is to protect yourself against losses that you may not be able to afford.

Now don't get all nervous and uptight about this. You don't have to get all this coverage right now. A good insurance plan is something that evolves over a lifetime. You build the structure a little at a time, adding pieces as you change and grow. When you're young and single, all you probably need is some auto insurance, basic residential, health, and disability. Married couples need to add some life insurance to the mix, and as families grow, they need more protection. So you see, insurance will fit into your life gradually, and by the time you're finished reading this book, you'll know exactly how.

Excuses, Excuses

You are creative—no more so than in those imaginative excuses you concoct to avoid the task of addressing your insurance needs. Here's a litany of typical excuses. They are provided to save you the trouble of listing ridiculous reasons yourself. Does any of this sound familiar?

- *"I don't have enough money."* You may feel adequate insurance is too expensive, that it is financially out of your reach. Like so many people, you are probably struggling today just to pay for your immediate needs. Most of your paycheck goes for paying down loans, paying off bills, and saving a little for a modest three-day outing with your friends or family. How in the world can you expect to pay for renter's insurance or a life insurance policy? Well, start thinking about what your life would be like if you came back from that three-day outing to discover that everything but your dirty laundry had been lifted from your home. If you had had enough home-owner's insurance, you'd have been covered.

• *"It's too complicated."* Oh puh-leaze. You maneuver through the World Wide Web. You can uncover the cheapest airfare from Indianapolis to Aspen in the middle of ski season. You can decipher the ingredients in a bottle of shampoo enough to know you don't want the stuff on your hair. If you can do that, you can understand the basics of just about any insur-ance policy you might need.

• *"My employer provides insurance so I don't have to worry about it."* Oh really? Your employer may provide insurance, but it may not be right for you. You won't know that, though, unless you have a pretty good understanding about insurance and what insurance belongs in your life. And even if your employer pays for all or part of the insurance, there may be choices within the plan. You need to know the basics so you can make intelligent decisions. Also, should you lose or leave your job, you may need to buy insurance on your own.

• *"The government eventually will pass universal health insurance, and I'll be covered. Meanwhile, Medicare or Medicaid automatically will pay for my health costs if I don't have insurance."* Lots of fallacies here. First, universal health care is not even on the political agenda for this century. Don't wait for something that may never become a reality. Second, Medicare is mostly for the elderly. Third, Medicaid is primarily for the poor. Fourth, if you are neither elderly nor poor and do not meet other, very specific qualifi-cations, you must pay all your medical costs or get insurance.

Profile Yourself

The key to understanding insurance is knowing what you need to insure, how you need to insure it, and for how much. Before you can make realistic choices about what kinds of insurance you need and how much, you should assess what's important to you. Your lifestyle will determine just how much protection is enough and how much it's going to cost. A 30-year-old woman pregnant with her first child is going to care about postnatal health insurance a lot more than a 22-year-old single guy. A first-time home buyer needs to know about homeowner's insurance, but is a lot less concerned with an umbrella liability policy than a married couple with three children, a house, a boat, and a motor home. A couple with four children is going to be more concerned with life insurance than a pair of young newlyweds. And the classic example: A single white male, 22 years of age, driving a 1995 Corvette, is going to pay a lot more for car insurance than a married 45-year-old mother of two driving a 1995 Ford Taurus.

Your goal should be to define what and who are most important to you and protect them against the consequences of unforeseen future events. So the first step is to take a good hard look at yourself. What's important to you? What do you have that's worth protecting? Make a list of all the things you couldn't afford to lose, and then imagine losing them. Then picture yourself making a phone call that sets the wheels in motion to get them all back. That's what home and auto insurance does.

And it may be unpleasant, but try to imagine your spouse's sudden passing. How will you continue to pay the mortgage and send the kids to college? In this case, insurance is an absolute necessity.

Insurance Self-Assessment

Take a look at the worksheet on page 6. The top row across lists the people you might want to protect with insurance. The column running down the left represents all of the unexpected costs and dangers from which you might want to protect yourself and your loved ones. Some of those are filled in and some have blanks for you to fill in. Add as many risks to this chart as you'd like. Then go through it and check off which risks you need to be protected from and whom you want to protect.

Great Moments in Insurance History

The concept of insurance is both simple and ancient. The idea of transferring the risk of loss from one person to a group began thousands of years ago. In communal tribal living, when a family's hut burned down, the entire tribe would rebuild it.

About 2500 B.C., Chinese merchants were using primitive forms of marine insurance. When boat operators reached a rapids in the river, they waited for other boats to arrive. Then, they redistributed the cargo so that each boat carried some of the contents of the others. If one boat was lost navigating the rapids, all the operators shared a small loss. That way, no one operator was wiped out.

About the same time in Egypt, insurance was available through benevolent societies. These were organized primarily for religious and social purposes. Members contributed to funds that paid burial expenses. Aid was also available to those who were seriously ill or injured by accident. Though the evidence is not conclusive, some historians believe that by 1500 B.C., these societies also provided fire insurance.

Risk	Yourself	Your Spouse	Your Children
Health expenses:			
Annual checkups	☐	☐	☐
Short-term hospital/medical costs	☐	☐	☐
Long-term hospital costs	☐	☐	☐
Prenatal care	☐	☐	☐
Psychiatric care	☐	☐	☐
Loss of income from a disability	☐	☐	☐
_____	☐	☐	☐
_____	☐	☐	☐
_____	☐	☐	☐
_____	☐	☐	☐
_____	☐	☐	☐
_____	☐	☐	☐
_____	☐	☐	☐
Property you want to protect:			
Home/apartment	☐	☐	☐
Furniture	☐	☐	☐
Furs	☐	☐	☐
Jewelry	☐	☐	☐
Business equipment	☐	☐	☐

Risk	Yourself	Your Spouse	Your Children
Auto	☐	☐	☐
_____	☐	☐	☐
_____	☐	☐	☐
_____	☐	☐	☐
_____	☐	☐	☐
_____	☐	☐	☐
_____	☐	☐	☐
_____	☐	☐	☐
_____	☐	☐	☐

Legal liability from which you need to protect yourself:

	Yourself	Your Spouse	Your Children
In your house	☐	☐	☐
On the grounds of your house	☐	☐	☐
Car accidents	☐	☐	☐
Damage to someone else's property	☐	☐	☐
_____	☐	☐	☐
_____	☐	☐	☐
_____	☐	☐	☐
_____	☐	☐	☐
_____	☐	☐	☐
_____	☐	☐	☐
_____	☐	☐	☐
_____	☐	☐	☐
_____	☐	☐	☐
_____	☐	☐	☐

MATCHING THE RISK WITH THE INSURANCE

You can get insurance to protect you from different types of risk. Take a look.

Risk/Type of Insurance

Premature death/Life
   insurance
Loss of earning
   power/Disability
   insurance
Unexpected
   expenses/Health and
   auto insurance
Loss of property/Auto and
   residential insurance
Legal liability/Auto and
   residential insurance

Now look at your list. What is important to you? Do you have people in your life who depend on you for the roof over their heads and the food on their table? If so, you need to consider life insurance to protect them if you die. If you drive a nice car, then you need to make sure you have enough collision and liability insurance on it. What about the stereo system in your apartment? Then renter's insurance should be a prime concern for you.

Remember, though, that as your lifestyle changes, so do your insurance needs. So it's important to reassess your situation regularly. The key is to understand the concepts that motivate your insurance coverage so you can mold the protections you've set up to fit your needs at any moment in time.

For instance, when you purchase your first home, you might want to buy extra life insurance to pay off your mortgage if you die. Once you've paid down most of your mortgage, you can eliminate this portion of the policy. Or if you're married with kids, be sure your employer's health insurance covers them, too. If not, you'll have to supplement it either by contributing to the plan, if you can, or getting some on your own.

The Nuts and Bolts

Now that you know what you want to insure, the question you need to answer is: How do you insure them, and for how much? Those are the keys to making the most of your insurance plan. Don't let the jargon intimidate you. This book will show you how to conquer the gibberish and maximize the countless insurance choices you will face along the way. Getting a clue about insurance means understanding what you can do now to protect yourself from the negative consequences of a future event. When you look at it that way, the reasons for purchasing insurance become clear:

- *You can't predict the future.* This is the reality that drives control freaks crazy and the rest of us to purchase some type of insurance. Thus, while you can't foresee what's going to happen, you can imagine various scenarios ranging from the outlandish (your home being transported to the planet Jupiter by little orange aliens) to the possible (a burglar lifting your television, VCR, and camcorder). Look back at the list you created earlier. What can't you afford to lose?

- *You want to protect yourself from the financial consequences of unpredictable but possible events.* This aspect of insurance is particularly important when it comes to the possibility that others might be hurt on your property or by things that belong to you. For example, what happens if your friend Mary slips on your hallway throw rug and breaks her arm? Without insurance, you would have to pay for her medical costs and, perhaps, compensate her out of your own pocket for any loss of income. That could be a big bill. Worse still, you might get hit with a lawsuit for hundreds of thousands of dollars. To protect yourself from these costs, you buy homeowner's insurance. The insurance company pays the bills—or at least most of them—not you.

BE PREPARED TO HAND OVER YOUR HISTORY

Checking Your Credit

After you apply for insurance—especially auto and casualty policies—many insurers will run a check on your credit. This helps them assess you as a risk.

The company will ask for your consent. You have the right to decline, but that will raise a red flag—and the company may decide not to issue the policy. If you give permission, and the company decides not to issue you a policy because of something in your credit history, you have the legal right to request a copy of your credit report free of charge. It's in your best interest to take advantage of the opportunity to make sure it's accurate.

- *You want peace of mind.* Knowing that you don't have to worry about the financial consequences of something bad happening to anything or anyone on your list ought to make you sleep a little better and perhaps even lower your blood pressure.

Life, Health, Auto, Home

Most things that can be insured fall into one of these four categories. And together, they make up your complete insurance shelter. Think of your insurance needs as the pieces or building blocks of a physical structure that protect you from different types of risk. That structure has:

- *A foundation and basement.* Although they aren't ideal, government entitlement programs like Social Security disability insurance can act as your insurance safety net. It's nice to know that your tax dollars are hard at work and that these programs exist, but just like a tightrope walker hopes he never has to fall into the net, you should hope that you never have to take advantage of these insurance options. We'll take you through the basics in chapter three.

- *Floors.* These are medical insurance policies that you purchase or that are provided by your employer. Without your health, nothing much else matters. From HMOs to private insurance companies, we'll guide you through the ins and outs of protecting yourself and your family in chapters four, five, and six.

- *Walls.* These are property/casualty policies that protect things such as your house or automobile. Your walls are also the liability policies that protect you from the financial consequences of damages that you may do to others, such as injuring someone while driving your car. Beginning in chapter seven, we'll show you how tall and how thick your walls should be.

- *A roof.* This is life insurance. It does a lot more than merely cover the cost of your funeral. The purpose of life insurance also involves providing financial resources for your family after you die. Life insurance is the cap on your protection, and we'll explain it all to you in chapter twelve.

The Right Stuff

Getting the right type of floors, walls, and roof for your insurance structure starts with this five-step process:

1. Get a general idea of the different types of insurance available and what they cover. You'll also want to get a handle on the jargon so you can talk to your insurance agent intelligently. For instance, you need to know what a deductible is and how it affects what you pay for your insurance.

2. Find out from whom you should buy your insurance. Learn how to compare different insurance agents and companies so you can make well-informed purchasing decisions.

3. Become familiar with the different types of provisions within a specific type of insurance. For instance, what do the standard home-owner's policies cover? It's to your advantage to know that while your policy probably covers the theft of your watch at the airport, it may not cover the theft of your laptop computer at that same airport. Most likely, you'll need additional coverage for that.

4. Assess your own insurance needs. Most people are either over- or underinsured. Once you get a clue, you'll be paying for exactly what you need.

5. Understand how to compare insurance policies. Primary rule: Always comparison shop for insurance. Policy prices and provisions can vary greatly from company to company.

ANSWERING ALL THOSE QUESTIONS

When it comes to insurance applications, honesty really is the best policy. Remember, when you buy insurance coverage, you're entering into a contract. If you misrepresent facts—fail to disclose a pre-existing condition or fib about an auto accident—you run the risk of voiding the contract and losing out on any benefits.

Don't Overengineer: It's a Plan— Not a Prison

You cannot plan for every eventuality in your life, so don't try to buy insurance for a dozen different scenarios. You don't walk out the door with 100 pounds of clothes and

BUILD YOUR INSURANCE STRUCTURE... ONE BRICK AT A TIME

If you have no insurance coverage at this point in your life and thinking about it all is giving you a case of information overload...relax! You don't have to know everything there is to know about insurance right away, and you don't have to buy every kind of coverage all at once. Just keep in mind that now is the time to start getting your insurance house in order. You can begin with some basic coverage now and add to the package as you go along. Think of total insurance protection as a work in progress, and use this book as your guide.

necessities for subzero weather and 110-degree afternoons alike, for hailstorms and icestorms, for hurricanes and earthquakes. Instead, dress for today's forecast. You may get drenched by a sudden rainstorm, but at least your burden is light enough to allow you to scurry for cover.

The same holds for insurance. Don't overload yourself with insurance policies that protect you against every possible thing that could happen. You work hard for your money. Don't waste it buying insurance you don't need. Your goal is to get the right mix of insurance at each stage of your life.

Time Passages

If You're:	You Need This Type of Insurance:	So That:
Single	Health	Your assets are not eaten up by health care costs.
		A hospital will not refuse to treat you.
	Disability	You have an income if you are injured and cannot work.
	Car	You have liability coverage if you have an accident and you are reimbursed if your car is damaged or stolen.
	Residential	Your valuables and your property are covered, as are liabilities for injuries.
Married/ no kids	All of the above + term life on you and spouse	You or spouse will have an income in case one of you dies.
Married with kids	All of the above + term life on you and spouse	You or spouse and children will have an income in case one of you dies.

Know Your Rights

How long is too long to wait for your benefit payment?

How soon you receive a benefit payment varies widely with the kind of insurance, the kind of loss, and the laws of the state where you live. For example, insurance companies usually wait at least 30 days before paying out for a stolen car in the hopes that the car will turn up. Life insurance claims can only be paid after the company receives an official death certificate. Small auto accident claims are often paid on the spot after the damage is estimated by an insurance adjuster.

Almost all states have guidelines that spell out the amount of time a company has to respond in writing to a claim and to pay a claim once a settlement has been reached. Unfortunately, though, these rules come complete with loopholes that allow insurers to delay at length if they question your claim.

On the bright side, though, insurers are usually eager to pay benefits, since delays only add to the cost of doing business.

How do I fight an "unfair" payment?

If you disagree with the insurance company's handling of your claim, you can and should take action. In most states, the process of appealing a claim is a series of increasingly confrontational steps:

1. Talk to your agent or claims manager. Explain your side, provide copies of supporting documents, and send copies of correspondence and documents to company executives (their address is usually on the first page of the policy).

2. Take advantage of government resources. If you're still not satisfied, most states have an insurance help line, arbitrators, and appeals process.

3. Hire an attorney. Using a lawyer to help you fight your case will cost you—either in fees or as a percentage of the eventual settlement or judgment. But sometimes only an attorney with experience dealing with recalcitrant insurance companies can get you a fair settlement.

CREATING an *insurance* BLUEPRINT

Before you build your insurance structure, you need to create the blueprint. Begin by mastering the lingo, and finish by constructing a clear-cut plan for your floors, walls, and roof.

To build a solid insurance framework—one that fits your needs and budget—you must start with a blueprint. To create that blueprint, you'll need to understand a few more basic concepts that underpin just about every type of insurance you might ever need. It will also help to understand how insurance companies and agents operate, as they are the contractors you'll be hiring.

What Is Insurance and Where Does It Come From?

You already know that insurance is something you buy in order to protect yourself, your family, and your possessions from unforeseen future events. But do you know where it comes from? And better yet, why anybody would want to sell it to you? It

doesn't seem logical that someone else would want to take responsibility for your losses, does it? Well, that's exactly what insurance companies want to do.

They want you to hand the responsibility over to them—for a fee, of course. Insurance companies are not in the business because they are benevolent. They're in it to make money. In fact, they're in it to make a lot of money. State Farm, the largest insurance company in this country, reported over $34 billion in earned premiums in 1996. State Farm also pays out billions of dollars in claims. Essentially, though, State Farm banks on the fact that they will take in more money in premiums than they will pay out in claims.

But insurance companies don't take many chances. They spend a lot of their time measuring risk, and risk determines who a company will insure and at what cost. For example, if you're a low risk, you'll be able to get insurance more easily, and you'll pay less for it than if you were a high risk.

So how is risk measured? It's very complicated, involves complex mathematical formulas, and uses lots and lots of different statistics. Fortunately, you don't need to know advanced algebra to grasp the idea behind measuring risk. It's based on the law of averages.

It's All about Profit

It's easier to understand how to use insurance once you see this equation from the point of view of the insurance companies.

They make their money in two ways:

1. If you want insurance, you pay for it, usually in equal monthly, quarterly, biannual, or annual payments, called premiums.

2. Once the insurance companies have your premiums, though, they don't just put them in the bank. While they keep a small amount of cash reserves (your state insurance commission requires it), they invest most of it in businesses, stocks, and real estate. (When Prudential talks about a piece of the rock, they're not kidding.) Insurance companies are even involved in mortgages and car financing.

Exclusive Agents with Direct Writers versus Independent Agents with Agency Firms

Keep in mind that exclusive representatives and agents sell insurance for direct insurance companies and only for one company. Independent agents sell for a number of different insurance companies.

So which type of agent—exclusive or independent—has the best insurance deal for you? Neither and both. It really depends on the insurance policy—and thus the company underwriting the policy—rather than the agent who is merely selling the policy.

Still, you should be prepared for the sales pitch you will get from each. The exclusive agent will tell you that the direct writer for which he sells can offer cheaper policies because they have their own sales force which sells directly to you. The independent agent will tell you it's to your advantage to buy from her because she can offer you a wider choice of policies.

Put such arguments aside. For you, the important things to consider are:

• The financial health of the insurance company underwriting the policy

• The complaint ratio, which indicates problems other consumers in your state have had with the underwriter

• How well the policy fits your needs

• The price—or premium—of the policy

Buying insurance is like buying a winter coat. You purchase according to quality and price. You don't care how the sales clerk is paid and you don't buy a coat that doesn't fit, no matter what the price. So it goes with buying insurance. Look for quality and insurance that fits your needs at the best possible price.

INSURANCE AGENTS VERSUS INSURANCE BROKERS

Insurance brokers are totally different from both exclusive and independent agents. Brokers represent buyers rather than sellers of insurance, and they usually handle commercial or business insurance rather than individual home, auto, health, or life insurance policies. For example, a manufacturer might hire a broker to find and negotiate an insurance policy to cover goods the company ships to a distributor.

By following the steps that this book provides, you act as your own broker and thus avoid this middleperson and the accompanying broker fees.

They spend money in four ways:

1. They pay claims. If you need to redo your bathroom tile because your upstairs neighbor's faulty pipes leaked, you ask your insurance company to pay for that by submitting a claim.

2. They employ armies of claims adjusters, supervisors, and accountants to check and double-check to be sure those claims are legitimate. If the word got out that it was easy to rip off insurance companies, everyone would do it. So they have to be forever vigilant that the claims they pay are righteous. It can cost hundreds of dollars or more to send out a check for $100. In fact, it costs as much or more to process a tiny claim as it does to process a multimillion-dollar life insurance payout.

3. They advertise and market their services. This is how they get the word out that they have different types of policies that cover different situations.

4. They pay commissions to the agents who sell their services. For some companies, the lion's share of the first year's premium goes straight to the agent. That explains why insurance agents seem so eager.

Insurance companies spend all their time trying to maximize their income and minimize their outgo. Managing the income from the investments they make is a big challenge because they need to be sure they have enough money available to pay for the inevitable claims, with lots left over for profits. Remember, an insurance company is a for-profit business!

One of the ways they minimize their outgo is by employing legions of people called actuaries. Using techniques so refined they call it a science, actuaries figure out the odds that the company will have to pay off a claim. They know that a left-handed smoker is more (or less) likely to have a head-on accident. They know that a fireman in Florida is more (or less) likely to have a heart attack. And they use these numbers to determine exactly what the premium ought to be so they can anticipate the payout and still make money.

Insurance companies actually are willing to lose a bit of money on the insurance part of their business, as long as they have their hands on the premiums long enough to make their investments pay off. But thanks to the actuaries and their number crunching, they usually make money on the insurance as well.

Insurance companies also try to increase profits by limiting the amount they pay out in claims. Some do this by aggressively uncovering fraud. Others (a minority) take the position that the consumer is going to have to fight to get any claims money. While some consumers view an insurance payment as a right due them with no questions asked, smart ones realize that they have to be prepared, in advance, for resistance.

A *New York Times* article reported that an insurance company held up a quadriplegic's benefits for 35 years, "waiting for me to die," as he described it. Insurance companies are heavily regulated, so such egregious acts are few and far between, but there's no question that some companies are more likely to cooperate than others. Checking out a company's payment history is the single most important thing you can do when comparing insurance companies. After all, the only reason you're buying the insurance is to get paid if something bad happens. Find a company that gladly and professionally pays claims.

So you see that in the short run, there's just no incentive for an insurance company to be eager to pay you the money you're due. But fortunately, the leading companies

Too Many Minor Claims

Nora changed car insurance companies last year on the advice of her agent, who found her a policy with lower premiums for the same coverage. She religiously paid her premiums on time to the new company, submitted all the proper documentation each time she filed a claim, and felt she was a solid citizen of the insurance market. So she was shocked at the end of the year when the insurance company refused to renew her policy.

What happened to Nora happened to a small percentage of insurance customers in New York State, and it could happen to you no matter where you live. Nora's problem was neither late payment nor nonpayment of premiums. It was too many claims.

Insurance companies might refuse to renew your policy if you submit what they perceive to be nuisance claims—frequent small claims that don't seem to amount to much, but that could have disastrous consequences. Their reasoning is that a person who has lots of minor fender benders, for example, poses too great a potential for eventually getting involved in a major accident requiring a huge payout. To preserve their rate structure—because they'll have to offset big payouts with an across-the-board increase in premiums—they have the right to drop customers who file claims too often, and they do exercise that right.

What's too often? Use good judgment here. Don't be afraid to submit legitimate claims, but don't go overboard. If you find yourself filing minor claims every few months, they may be considered excessive and you might be taking a chance that your policy won't be renewed. You should also evaluate *why* you are filing so many claims—do you need to improve your driving?

have realized that in the long run, if they don't pay off, people are going to stop buying insurance. That's why you'll see ads about eager adjusters who head out to floods and natural disasters, checkbook in hand.

That leads to the third big cost insurance companies face: marketing. They spend billions of dollars on advertising and direct mail. A long time ago, insurance companies discovered that people didn't really want to buy insurance, that it needed to be sold. A company that does a better selling job ends up with more people insured. Higher demand means they can charge higher rates, which translates to more profits.

The more advertised and therefore the more convenient a policy appears to be for you to buy, the more the insurance company paid to market it. And while volume can sometimes lead to better efficiency and lower prices, more often than not, just like the advertised brand in the supermarket, the cost of advertising gets passed on to the consumer in the form of higher prices. Shop around, a lot. Usually, the more accessible insurance is, the more it costs.

So, yes, the insurance companies are in it for the profits—this is America, after all—but knowing this fact shouldn't discourage you from buying insurance. Profits aside, the insurance companies provide a valuable service—protecting you from huge losses you can't afford. You don't stay away from dry cleaners or supermarkets because they're in business to make money. Don't turn away from all forms of insurance because the insurance company is using your money to increase profits.

The Vocabulary

Now that you know why insurance companies do what they do, it's time to take a look at some of the language you'll need to understand before delving into your actual coverage. These are the tools in the well-supplied toolbelt you'll wear while you build your insurance structure.

- *Premium.* The premium is the price you pay the insurance company for a specific type of insurance policy. The premium is determined by the thing you want to insure (a $100,000 frame house versus a $500,000 brick

home), the events that could happen to that thing (fires, windstorms, and earthquakes), and the dollar level of insurance you want ($50,000 to replace the frame house or $300,000 to replace the brick one). The important thing to keep in mind is that premiums charged by different insurance companies, for the exact same coverage, can vary by more than 100 percent. Thus, when you compare premiums, make sure the insurance coverage is the same.

- *Deductible.* Most insurance policies do not cover the entire financial cost of what is being insured. Let's take the example of a tree falling on your house, and the cost to repair the roof is $3,500. You may have to pay $500 of that $3,500 out of your own pocket. That $500 you pay before the insurance coverage kicks in is called your deductible. All insurance policies have deductibles. The higher your deductible, the lower your premium, and vice versa. A good rule of thumb is to buy the policy with the highest deductible you can afford to pay. So if you think you can afford to pay $1,000 of that roof repair, choose a $1,000 deductible. That way you'll be paying lower monthly premiums.

- *Claim.* A claim is the request you make to the insurance company to reimburse you for a loss you have had that is covered by a policy. The most common claim is a first-party claim, which involves collecting on a policy that you have purchased. You smash your car into a cement wall and collect money from the insurance company to help pay for the auto repairs. A third-party claim involves collecting from someone else's insurance company. Let's say someone smashes his car into your cement wall. You then collect from the company which insures that driver for the damage he did to your wall.

- *Underwriter.* This is the insurance company that creates the insurance policy. The underwriter sets the terms and premiums of the policy. If you buy a policy and then make a claim, it is the underwriter—the insurance company—that pays you.

Stock versus Mutual Insurance Companies

Insurance salespeople love to tell you why the insurance companies they represent are the best. Some agents will extol the virtues of being a publicly-held—a.k.a. stock—company. Others will tell you how lucky you will be to have your insurance with a mutual insurance company.

The reality is that the financial health of the company and its operating record in the state where you live are far more important guideposts than whether it's a stock or mutual company. There are small nuances, though. Here are the differences.

• *Stock insurance firms.* These companies are owned by one or more investors. When the company makes money, the investors may receive a portion of the profits in the form of a dividend. The company's stock may be traded on a stock exchange. As a policyholder, you do not get to share in the profits.

• *Mutual insurance companies.* These companies are owned by the policyholders. Thus, when you purchase auto insurance from a mutual company, you become a shareholder of that company. You get to share the profits—when there are profits.

Most insurance companies are stock firms. Examples are: Allstate, CNA, and Zurich American.

The Insurance Contract in Plain English

An insurance policy is a legal contract, and every contract contains four basic components:

1. One person (or party, in legal parlance) must make an offer, and the other must accept it.

2. Both parties must be of legal signing age and mentally competent.

3. The subject matter or activity covered in the contract must be legal.

4. Each party must assume some obligation toward the other or give something of value—like money or a promise—to the other.

So how does this work with an insurance contract? The insurance company makes an offer—to provide auto insurance, for instance—to you. Let's say you sign the insurance policy. Now, assuming you are old enough and not insane, you must follow the rules and procedures in the policy. You must also pay the company some money—a premium—for the insurance. In return, the company must pay you for certain costs if you have an auto accident and if those costs were spelled out in the contract.

- *Policyholder*. That's you. The insurance company—the underwriter—creates a policy. If you choose to buy it, you pay the premiums. Then, you hold the policy.

- *Rider*. This is a special provision that is added to—or "rides" on—an insurance policy. Riders can expand or limit the benefits paid to you when you make a claim. Some riders allow you to renew your policy under certain conditions. For instance, a guaranteed purchase rider on a life insurance policy might let you increase the coverage of the policy from a $250,000 death benefit to a $500,000 death benefit without first taking a medical exam. Most policies send you to the doctor before letting you increase your coverage. There are literally hundreds of riders that can be added onto the various insurance policies you may hold. We'll walk you through most of the options later on.

- *Floater*. This is a type of insurance policy that covers property that can be moved—such as jewelry, artwork, or sports equipment. Thus, the insurance coverage "floats" with the insured item whether you leave it at home or take it on vacation.

PREMIUM OPTIONS

Most insurance policies have a one-year premium, but paying the whole thing in one lump can be difficult. That's why almost all insurers allow you to pay in installments—usually monthly or quarterly.

Of course, there's a hook: You'll pay a small fee—a dollar or two per month, or sometimes an interest charge—for the convenience of an installment plan. If your insurance company doesn't tack on such costs, take advantage of it. It's like receiving an interest-free loan.

Slow Ahead for Risk, Peril, and Hazard

Three major concepts—risk, peril, and hazard—pervade the insurance universe. Sure you know what these three mean when it comes to taking a risk, protecting yourself from perils you might encounter on a hiking trip, and just avoiding the daily hazards on the highway. In the world of insurance, these terms have very specific meanings.

GREAT MOMENTS IN INSURANCE HISTORY

The biblical Joseph, with his amazing coat of many colors, provides another early example of insurance principles. Around 1500 to 1700 B.C., according to historians, Joseph interpreted a dream of the Egyptian Pharaoh to mean that there would be seven years of plenty followed by seven years of famine. At Joseph's suggestion, the Egyptians set aside grain during the years of plenty to prepare for the years of famine. Today, people set aside a little now to protect themselves against possible future emergency or loss.

Throughout this book, we'll be using the word risk according to its real-world definition, meaning a chance of loss or injury. But the insurance company refers to you as a risk. In other words, the insurance company considers the thing that is at stake—you, your car, your house—to be the risk, not the activity that causes you, your car, or your house to be injured or damaged. Thus, auto accidents, hurricanes, and broken bones are not risks, according to insurance companies. The person or the property insured is the risk, because that person or property could sustain a loss. So how does it feel to be a risk? Like something that needs insurance?

Peril is the cause of the loss. It is what you are insuring the risk against. People buy insurance policies for financial protection against such perils as auto accidents, hurricanes, and broken bones. Insurance policies stipulate what perils they cover and which ones they don't. For instance, a flood is one peril that is not covered by the standard homeowner's policy. Windstorms, though, are perils that are routinely covered.

A hazard increases the likelihood of loss due to a peril. For example, if you have bad brakes on your car, it increases the likelihood that you will have an accident. If there is a diseased and decaying tree hanging over your house, it increases the likelihood that a branch will fall and damage the roof. If you smoke two packs of cigarettes a day, it increases the likelihood that you will develop emphysema or die of lung cancer.

Control the Hazard, Cut the Cost

Hazards come in all shapes and sizes. Some are more hazardous than others. By eliminating hazards, you can usually decrease the cost of insurance. Lock your car in a garage

rather than parking it on the street and you can lower the cost of your auto insurance. Let's take a look at four major categories of hazards. Notice how you can control some of them more easily than others.

Physical Hazards

Physical hazards refer to the physical characteristics or conditions of the thing that is insured. Fix the faulty wiring in the handyman's special you're buying, and you can cut your homeowner's insurance cost. For some physical hazards, though, you have little control. You will pay more for insurance on a frame house than a brick house because a frame house burns more easily than a brick house.

CAN YOU GET A REFUND IF YOU DON'T USE THE POLICY?

If you cancel a policy after paying the premium, you should get a refund for the unused but paid-for term. You won't get money back for the period the policy was in force.

If your home is located in a high crime area, you may also pay more than if you lived in a lower-crime-rated neighborhood. In such a case, there's not much you can do to lower your insurance cost other than to install a security system to keep the burglars out and to work with your community groups to make the area safer. Unfortunately, that security system may cost a pretty penny and not even lower your insurance bill that much.

Moral Hazards

Moral hazards involve your own behavior. They refer to things that you might intentionally do to increase the likelihood of loss, therefore forcing the insurance company to pay out money to you. A moral hazard would exist if you insured your house for $500,000 even though it was only worth a maximum of $150,000. In such a situation, you could profit mightily should your home burn to the ground. The insurance company will eliminate the moral hazard by preventing you from insuring your house for more than the $150,000 it is worth.

It's also a moral hazard if your insurance company pays your family benefits from your life insurance policy if you take your own life. Most life insurance companies won't pay your survivors if you commit suicide within two years after the policy is issued.

Take the Pulse of Your Insurance Company to Check Up on Its Health

Before you fork over any premiums, see if your insurer is healthy. You don't want to pay a low premium only to turn on the evening news two months from now and learn that your insurer is barreling down the road to bankruptcy. Consult the ratings published by at least one of the four independent firms. Many of these are available at your public library or at a Web site. Remember, these ratings companies cover an insurance firm's financial health, not its service.

A. M. Best
Ambest Rd.
Oldwick, NJ 08858
(908) 439-2200
Fax: (908) 439-2433
Web site: http://www.ambest.com

Standard & Poor's
25 Broadway
New York, NY 10004
(212) 208-8000
Fax: (212) 412-0475
Web site: http://www.ratings.com

Duff & Phelps Credit Rating
311 South Wacker Dr.
Chicago, IL 60606
(312) 697-4600
Fax: (312) 697-0112
Web site: http://www.duffllc.com

Weiss Ratings
4176 Burns Rd.
Palm Beach Gardens, FL 33410
(800) 289-9222
Fax: (561) 625-6685
Web site: http://www.weissratings.com

Moody's Investor Service
99 Church St.
New York, NY 10007
(212) 553-0300
Fax: (212) 553-4558
Web site: http://www.moodys.com

The moral hazard issue is the reason insurers require you to agree in writing to any insurance policy that covers your life. This reduces the moral hazard of murder. Think about it. Why would anyone want to insure your life without you knowing about it? The answer is that this person must have some devious plans for you.

The insurance company—not you—determines moral hazard. The insurance company will not issue a policy that might tempt you to do something illegal or immoral in order to collect benefits. In addition, insurers may refuse to issue you a policy if they think your morality is questionable, making it more likely that you'll commit a moral hazard—like arson—in order to collect insurance. If your previous history or actions raise questions about your morality, the insurance company may not want to take the risk of insuring you.

Occupational Hazards

Because of occupational hazards, your job can raise the cost of your health insurance and life insurance. Firefighters are more likely to die than accountants because their jobs are more dangerous. When an employer pays a worker to perform a dangerous job, that worker should make sure that both the health insurance and life insurance that the employer offers are substantial. In this case, the employer should foot the bill for the increased cost of both the health and life insurance for these danger zone workers, and in fact, most of them do.

Your job doesn't have to be dangerous, though, to present a hazard to your health. Office workers—particularly those who work long hours on computers—are susceptible to a number of physical ailments such as carpal tunnel syndrome, backaches, and

WHY NOT OVERINSURE?

If insurance is a bet, are you allowed to make as big a bet as you want? Can you insure your car for a million dollars, or your favorite teddy bear for $1,000?

Not usually. The insurance policy almost always has a clause that prohibits you from collecting more than the thing is worth. Sometimes it's the replacement cost (buying a brand-new one), and sometimes it's the market value. So while an agent might let you buy a policy for a whole bunch of money (he makes the commission whether or not you collect), you collect the amount the policy says in the fine print. So save yourself from big disappointment. Don't overinsure.

Go for the Biggest Deductible You Can Afford to Lose

Insurance companies hate paying any claims, but it's the small ones that really annoy them. The amount they pay out isn't enough to give them good marketing word of mouth, or justify the amount of money it costs to process the claim. You can use this to your advantage to save a lot of money.

The reason for insurance is not to protect you from little losses. It's for the big stuff—the catastrophes and disasters. A deductible makes it easier for you to buy just that sort of insurance. Remember, if you're in a car accident, you pay the first $500 of the repair bill if you have a $500 deductible.

Always choose the biggest deductible that the insurance company will sell you and that you can afford to pay. You're buying car insurance for the $450,000 you might get sued for, not the $200 to fix your windshield, and you're buying homeowner's insurance in case the house burns down, not to fix your broken window.

Ideally, you'd want the deductible to be zero. But the price is not the same: Higher deductibles almost always result in lower premiums. In addition to saving the insurance companies from nuisance claims, higher deductibles allow you to build up strong moral hazard protection. Insurance companies know that if you're on the hook for the first $1,000, you're only going to get the important stuff fixed. For example, that dented bumper might not look so bad—for $300, you'd rather live with it. The insurance company likes that. It saves them money when they don't have to process your claim.

If you learn two things from this book, they should be these two rules:

1. Make sure your big risks (all of them) are insured.

2. Don't pay to insure little risks.

eyestrain. Check your health insurance policy to see if these and other health problems you might have are covered by the company insurance policy. It's also a good idea to practice preventive medicine by using ergonomically correct keyboards, chairs, and desks.

Recreational Hazards

This is the last type of hazard in the insurance business. You are the one who must pay the extra cost for insurance if your hobby or favorite leisure activity is particularly dangerous. If you're an aerobatic flyer or a racecar driver, you'll pay a lot more for insurance.

Real World Risk

When it comes right down to it, risk (actually "peril" in insurance lingo) is the key to understanding insurance premiums and payouts. Insurance companies spend most of their time evaluating risk—that is, when they're not busy writing policies and collecting premiums.

Assessing the risks you and your family face in day-to-day living is the key to building a secure insurance structure. The risk of your death requires life insurance if you have a family that depends on your economic support. The risk that your child may need surgery and rehabilitation services requires that you have health insurance. The risk that you or someone in your family may be sued because you or they accidentally killed someone while driving a car requires automobile bodily injury liability insurance.

Remember: You—not the insurance company—must determine the specific risks in your life. Your Insurance Self-Assessment Worksheet (chapter one) provides the basis for the blueprint for your total insurance structure. Once you have identified the risks that are specific to you and your family, you can start building the insurance structure that will protect you from the financial consequences of those risks.

Insurance companies get into the act with their own risk assessments to determine how much they will charge you for the insurance you want. They use risk

LLOYD'S OF LONDON

Lloyd's has entered the popular culture by becoming known as the insurance company that will insure anything. Actually, it's not an insurance company. Lloyd's is an association of (mostly) rich men, who personally take insurance risks. Someone looking to insure Columbus's voyage to the New World, for example, would have presented the risk to the folks at Lloyd's. If any one of them had wanted personally to underwrite the venture, he would have volunteered, and, individually or with others, would have used his personal wealth to guarantee the voyage.

This way of operating is so risky that a series of bad decisions almost wiped Lloyd's out a few years ago. In spite of the riskiness of what the firm does, it still insures almost anything. It's even insured Betty Grable's legs and Bruce Springsteen's voice. So if you want to insure your eyebrows for a few million bucks, give Lloyd's a call.

measurements to set their premiums. They gather lots of data about perils and hazards and use the information to predict how often certain types of losses occur.

Knowing how often something happens on average, the insurance company then sets a price for insuring that something. The more information an insurance company gathers about a risk or peril or hazard, the more accurate the prediction. For example, insurance companies know that young men in their twenties have more car accidents than any other demographic group. They know this because they've spent many years collecting data about car accidents. Therefore, when 22-year-old Michael applies for car insurance, he's going to get socked with a huge premium, even though he's never had an accident or received a ticket. Why? Because he's in a demographic group that the insurance industry has labeled "high-risk." As he gets older, though, his premiums will decrease until they stabilize at age 29.

Seems unfair? Maybe so. But remember, insurance companies know that—on average—they're more apt to have to pay a claim for a 22-year-old male than for a 22-year-old female. So, the guy is going to pay higher premiums. That's just a fact. But there's even more to it than that. The insurance company that does insure Michael is going to try to insure him along with a whole bunch of low-risk drivers in the hope of minimizing the risk that Michael represents. That's known as spreading the risk.

Spreading the Risk

Accurate information—and lots of it—is the main ingredient that insurance companies use for the formula to measure risk. The next step in baking the insurance pie is to spread, spread, spread the well-measured risk.

Next to measuring risk, insurance companies really like spreading it. Imagine a line of 10,000 people all waiting to buy homeowner's insurance. The insurance company needs to find a way to insure all of those people in a way that's both fair and profitable. They do this by grouping lower-risk people with some who are higher-risk into groups called risk pools. In that way, they are able to collect premiums from all of the people in the group, but hope that they will only have to pay out claims to some of them. Insurance companies most often use demographics and geography to group people.

So, let's look again at 22-year-old Michael. We've already seen that he's going to pay through the nose for auto insurance. However, when he gets ready to buy a home, he's going to be in a better situation than most because he lives in a safe neighborhood in the Northeast, a region of the country not usually threatened by natural disasters. He'll probably pay an average homeowner's premium.

The Three Key Rules

Which types of insurance are sensible, and which should you avoid like the plague? If you start thinking about insurance from the insurance company's point of view, the picture will become a lot clearer.

Insurance companies want you to see them as your protectors. TV commercials depict insurance agents racing to the rescue after someone has been rushed to the hospital or suffered an automobile accident. The insurance company is trying to send you a message: "Don't worry. Just buy our insurance, and we'll take care of you."

But as we have seen, insurance companies aren't in business to take care of you—they're trying to make money. They want to sell you as much insurance as they possibly can, whether or not you need it. In fact, the less likely it is that you'll collect that insurance, the better it is for them, because then they get to hold on to your money. So don't let insurance companies play on your worst fears. Instead, carefully evaluate

the pros and cons of each kind of insurance. There are definitely risks worth insuring—but there are also some types of insurance which you should avoid. These three rules should help you beat the insurance companies at their own game:

Rule #1

Don't insure small, unusual risks. Policies like auto earthquake insurance (especially if you live in Idaho) or rainy day vacation insurance are generally a waste of money. It's very unlikely that your car is going to be wiped out by an earthquake. But even if you're incredibly unlucky and this does happen, it won't bankrupt you. It's a risk that's not worth covering by insurance. (Unless of course you have a very expensive or rare car. Then you actually might want to consider insuring it against everything.) Same goes for vacation insurance. Why waste money on a premium for a small inconvenience that might or might not occur? If it really does rain on your trip to Arizona, then you can use the money that you would have spent on the premium to pay for indoor activities, like seeing movies.

Rule #2

Avoid "convenient" ways of buying insurance, like purchasing flight insurance from that box in the airport, or signing up for the rental car insurance policy offered to you at the rental car counter. Insurance companies know that impulses strike consumers when they are the most vulnerable and that it's an easy, almost irresistible way for you to buy insurance. As a result, they know that even if they charge more, you'll still be likely to buy it. Don't fall into this trap. First of all, these types of insurance are almost always unnecessary. The possibility that your plane will crash is slim, and the auto insurance you already have on your car at home will most likely cover you for the few days you use the rental car. But if you really do feel the need to buy extra insurance for these kinds of risks, do your homework in advance. Purchase flight insurance or car rental insurance from your regular insurance agent before you leave for your trip. You'll pay much less and will make a more informed decision. Insurance should never be an impulse buy.

Rule #3

The fewer claims an insurance company pays, the higher its profits. Face it. When looking at an expensive claim, most insurance companies are going to spend extra time to make sure the claim is valid. So take the time to understand the fine print of any policy you're considering. If it seems too good to be true, it probably is.

The most important thing you can do, though, is to make it very difficult for your insurance company to weasel out of paying your claim. Stacy, a 24-year-old journalist, recently purchased a deluxe, 64-inch color TV. A week later, her apartment was burglarized, and the TV was taken. Unfortunately, when she filed her insurance claim, she had no proof that she'd ever owned this expensive TV. She couldn't find the receipt, and didn't have any photos showing the TV sitting in her living room. The result? The insurance company refused to cover it and gave her $250, their standard payout on a stolen television set.

The best way to protect yourself against unfair denials is to document everything. Take photos or make videotapes of your belongings, and save all of your receipts. Once you have auto insurance, make sure that you take a picture of your car and document any incident or problem on the road. And for your health insurance policy, you should save all of your medical receipts, bills, and other records of expenses. Throughout this book, there will be lists for you to inventory your possessions. Use them! This way, you're laying the necessary groundwork to collect if your insurance company unfairly denies a claim. To protect your records (or copies of them), keep them in a safe place—a fireproof, locked box, in a safe, or with a friend or relative.

Where Do You Buy It?

There are several different sources from which you can buy your insurance. The yellow pages are filled with listings. Use the Internet to access the Web site for the Insurance News Network (http://www.insure.com) where you'll find extensive listings of auto, home, health, and life insurance companies. Your bank or stockbroker may also be able to sell you insurance. Or check to see if you can get insurance through a professional organization or association you belong to. The college from which you earned your degree and the religious institution where you worship are two other places that may offer insurance, usually at a discount.

Insurance agents sell insurance. Insurance companies create—or in industry parlance, write—insurance policies. Some agents sell similar insurance policies for a number of different insurance companies. Others sell for only one insurance company.

The important thing to remember when you go shopping for insurance is that it is the insurance company—not the agent—that sets the terms and price of the policy and pays the claims. When it comes time for you to collect on a claim, it is the insurance company—not the agent—that writes the check covering the losses that have been insured.

Therefore, there are three things you need to know about your insurance company before you buy a policy:

1. Will the company pay your claims?

2. How difficult is the company to work with? How often do people have to take legal action to get their claims paid?

3. Is the company going to last until the time you need to file a claim?

You can get answers to the first two questions from a regulator. The insurance industry is regulated on a state rather than a federal level, so contact the insurance regulator in your state. (See the resources section of this book for a list of regulators.)

Here's the telling question: What's the record of complaints—specifically the complaint ratio—for the insurance company? High complaint ratios indicate the company is making too many of its policyholders unhappy. You want to do business with a company that has a low complaint ratio relative to other companies on the list. The ratings services and the Better Business Bureau can give you this information. In addition, *Consumer Reports* magazine rates insurance companies. Call (914) 378-2000 to see which issue to consult.

You also need to know about the financial health of the insurance company that creates or writes the policy you want to buy. That's because financially healthy insurance companies have enough dollars in the corporate vault to pay the claims you make on them and to pay those claims promptly.

Fortunately, there are companies called rating services that issue report cards on the thousands of different insurance companies operating in the United States. These rating services use different criteria and grading systems, but they all issue A-B-C–type grades. An easy way to sift through your many choices is to eliminate any insurance company that does not sport an "A" on its report card. Keep the A-list handy. If a company is not on that list, do not even consider any policy written by such an insurance firm.

Insurance companies are differentiated not only by financial health and complaint factors, but also by how the insurance they create is sold. They fall into two categories— direct writers or indirect writers.

Direct writers employ representatives or agents who are paid salaries or commissions or some combination of the two. State Farm and Allstate are two of the biggest direct writers in the United States. Sometimes called exclusive agents, salespeople for these companies sell insurance policies only for these companies.

A subcategory of direct writers are direct marketers, who sell only through the mail or over the phone. Examples of such direct marketers are USAA (800) 531-8100 and GEICO (800) 841-3000.

Indirect companies—also known as agency companies—do not have their own salespeople. Examples of agency companies are Travelers Property & Casualty, Cigna, and the St. Paul Companies. Agency companies rely on independent insurance agents to sell the insurance policies that they create. The independent agents can sell the same type of insurance policies for a number of different companies, and they earn commissions from the insurance companies based on the amount of insurance they sell for each.

Be forewarned: When you check out the "Insurance" heading in the yellow pages, you will discover that direct writers with their exclusive agents are lumped together with indirect writers and the independent agents who sell their insurance products.

To determine which type of agent—and thus insurance company—you are speaking to, just ask this question: "Do you sell insurance for more than one company?" If the answer is "yes," you are dealing with an independent agent who sells for an indirect or agency insurance company. A "no" answer tells you that you are speaking to an exclusive agent of a direct writer.

The Blueprint

Now that you know the basics, it's time to grab your pencils and go to your drafting table to work up your insurance blueprint. Return to your Insurance Self-Assessment Worksheet. The needs you identified there provide the plans for the total insurance framework you'll create to protect you from the risks you and your family face.

Your insurance-building toolbelt is full. You know all about risk, peril, and hazard. You're also familiar with the terms—premium, deductibles, riders, and benefits—that salespeople will be using when you shop for the materials to construct your framework.

Most importantly, you know how to begin to evaluate the materials: the insurance policies offered. You will look for high quality and policies that serve your needs. Then you'll pick the policies with the best price.

THE *basic safety* NET

Take a brief look at Uncle Sam's safety net insurance. You can't rely on them for all of your insurance needs. But you need to know they're there because although they won't supply you with huge amounts of money, they may provide for your basic needs if you suffer a loss of income.

The biggest government insurance program is Social Security, mandated by the Federal Insurance Contributions Act (FICA), which most people think of as a retirement plan. In addition to retirement benefits, though, Social Security has a network of insurance programs—disability, life (survivor's benefits), and health (Medicare)—that can supply you with enough money to put food on the table and a roof over your head if your earning power is destroyed by illness or injury, for example, or if the main breadwinner in your family dies. Social Security should not be your only source of

GREAT MOMENTS IN INSURANCE HISTORY

Ancient Romans had both life and health insurance. The Collegia, which were Roman benevolent societies, paid the burial costs of their members out of monthly dues that were collected. These societies also provided financial help for the sick and aged. These payments represent early forms of old-age pension and disability insurance.

Roman guilds issued life insurance contracts for members. In A.D.225, a Roman by the name of Ulpian compiled a mortality—a.k.a. an annuity—table, which the government of Tuscany used well into the nineteenth century.

insurance—you need to supplement it with a full complement of private insurance policies—because Social Security payments may be enough to keep you going, but not too far.

Although collecting Social Security retirement benefits and taking advantage of Medicare are probably on your very far horizon, you or a member of your family may be eligible to receive benefits from the other parts of the Social Security program if you have worked and paid FICA taxes. If your spouse dies, you and your children may be eligible for survivor's benefits. If you become disabled under the eligibility standards of Social Security, you can collect a monthly check.

Do You Qualify for Social Security?

Social Security retirement benefits are based on a system of quarters of years. You qualify to receive benefits if you have worked 40 of these quarters or a total of ten years calculated in quarters. You can also qualify if you've worked less than ten years if you've earned a certain amount of money each year. In 1996, for example, if you earned $640, it was the equivalent of one Social Security quarter.

Although these guidelines do change from time to time, you can find out how many quarters you've accumulated by calling Social Security at (800) 772-1213 and asking them for a benefit estimate request. They'll send you the appropriate form. Fill it out and send it in. The Social Security Administration will send you back an estimate of the retirement benefits you should receive.

How Social Security Disability Can Help

Take a look at what happened to Mary, 25, and Jeff, 26, a married couple with two young kids. Mary worked 15 hours a week as an administrative assistant and used the income to pay for child care and groceries. Jeff was a sales rep for a wine distributor. Jeff's company provided health benefits but no life insurance. Mary's employer offered neither. Jeff slipped down a flight of stairs one night, fractured his back, and was unable to work for 13 months. Mary's salary wasn't enough to pay all the bills, but between the Social Security disability benefits and the disability policy from their insurance company, the family was able to stay afloat until Jeff was able to return to work.

Social Security assumes you do have additional sources of insurance, so don't plan to rely on this for your sole source of support. For instance, if you were married with a child and had a salary of $30,000 in 1995, and you became disabled in 1996, you would have been able to draw a monthly disability check from the government for $1,580 if you had met the eligibility requirements. Chapter six will fill you in on the disability insurance details.

Survivor's Benefits Can Help Pick Up the Pieces

Take a look at how Social Security survivor's benefits helped the Dawsons. Rebecca and Greg were in their thirties and had two children, ages 9 and 12. Both Rebecca and Greg worked: Rebecca earned $40,000 as a freelance editor working at home and paid her required FICA taxes. Greg brought in $37,000 as an internal bank auditor, a job which required that he travel to individual banks in a five-state area to examine their financial records.

Their comfortable existence was shattered when Rebecca developed ovarian cancer. While the medical benefits through Greg's employer paid the doctor bills, Rebecca was unable to work during the last 11 months of her life. After she died, Greg had to pay someone to care for the children while he went out of town working.

Social Security survivor's benefits helped to keep this whole scenario under financial control. Because Rebecca had worked and paid into the Social Security insurance system for over 40 quarters, Greg was eligible to receive about $900 a month on behalf of

Contacting Social Security

Getting information about any and all of the Social Security programs, your status, and your eligibility is fairly simple. To handle questions about retirement, disability, and survivor's benefits as well as Medicare, the Social Security program has offices in cities and towns throughout America. The nearest offices will be listed in your local telephone directory.

You also can contact the Social Security Administration headquarters 24 hours a day at (800) 772-1213. You can get general information about Social Security from the Internet (http://www.ssa.gov).

If you are confused or getting the runaround, don't hesitate to contact your U.S. senators or your U.S. congressional representative. Their staffs may be able to help you avoid the office-to-office telephone transfers you may encounter by giving you the precise phone number you need to get your questions answered and your problems solved.

If you do plug into Capitol Hill clout, make sure you:

• Write a brief thank-you note to the staff. This documents that you had a problem.

• Mention to the folks at the Social Security Administration that "Senator Joan Doe's office said you would be able to help me." Such phrases do make bureaucrats listen more intently.

each child (for a total of about $1,800 a month) from Social Security. These payments will continue until the kids are 18 years old and will help to pay a caregiver for the children as well as to replace some of the income Rebecca brought into the family.

Building a Sound Foundation

Remember, Social Security is an insurance program for America's working citizens. When you work, you pay your FICA taxes, which is like paying premiums for a private insurance policy. Of course, to reap the benefits you must pay into the program. If you are in business for yourself, make sure you are paying what you should be to FICA.

If you work for someone else who is deducting for FICA from your paycheck, it's a good idea to check every couple of years that your contributions—calculated by quarters of a year—match the records of the Social Security Administration. Employers have been known to make paperwork mistakes or, worse still, to deduct the FICA taxes but not forward them to the government.

So keep your pay stubs in a safe place. If there is any discrepancy between what you have paid to FICA and the number of credit quarters you think you have, then you will have the proof at your fingertips.

Do be sure to keep track of what survivor's benefits may be provided for your children if you die. This should be factored into the calculations you make when considering the level of life insurance you need to provide for your family.

Your Employer's Medical Plan: In or Out?

You may be able to choose not to be covered by your employer's health plan. Why would you want to do that? Well, perhaps your spouse's plan already covers you, or you already have coverage from a previous employer.

Some employers will give you the option of refusing their health benefits plan. Usually, if you want to do that, you will have to put it in writing. Often, though, you will not be able to refuse to be covered. The reason is that your employer may have a contract with an insurer to provide health benefits to "all" employees.

Compare your plan with your spouse's plan. If you have children, decide which plan best covers them. The spouse with the best plan puts the kids on that plan. If your spouse's plan can cover you and it is significantly more generous than your plan is, get covered with your spouse's plan and continue to keep the one with your employer if that is mandatory. Then your spouse's plan becomes what's known as your primary coverage and your employer's plan becomes your secondary coverage. You file claims with your primary carrier first and whatever they don't pay gets sent to your secondary carrier. Hopefully, they'll pick up the difference. In this case, though, make sure you are the only one covered by your employer's plan. There is no reason to pay to have your spouse or children covered by your plan, since they already are covered by your spouse's plan.

THE BRAVE *new* world of *health* INSURANCE

Now that you have a firm foundation, it's time to put in the floors of your insurance structure. The key to choosing the right health insurance is understanding what the options are and matching them up with your own needs.

The first time you probably had to consider health insurance was when you started your first job. Until then, you just went to the doctor and let Mom and Dad take care of it. It may be a rude awakening to realize that you're suddenly responsible for handling your own medical bills, but this doesn't have to be as daunting as it first seems. After all, health insurance exists as a support mechanism for you, to make sure that you'll be able to afford medical care if and when you need it. The key is to understand the terminology well enough so that you can make an informed decision about what kind of coverage is best for you.

This book provides you with the tools you need to sort through and evaluate your options. If your employer offers just one plan, you'll still want to understand just what is and is not covered. If you have a choice of plans at your workplace, you'll want to

HOW MUCH OF YOUR HEALTH CARE COSTS CAN YOU DEDUCT ON YOUR TAX RETURN?

If you are self-employed you can deduct up to 40 percent of your health care premium in 1997. That percentage will increase year by year until 2006, when you'll be able to deduct 80 percent of the premium. If your employer pays for part, it's unlikely you can deduct anything. Check with your tax preparer.

be able to compare them so you can pick the one that's best for you and other members of your family. And of course, if you need to buy an individual policy, you'll want to have a thorough understanding of what's available.

Health insurance is something that every adult needs to think about on a regular basis. Even if you're already in a health insurance plan, you should be continually re-evaluating your options. After all, the medical needs of a 22-year-old single woman are very different from those of a 35-year-old married woman who's pregnant with her first child. As you enter different stages of life, you will almost definitely want to make changes in your health insurance plan, in order to make it more responsive to your needs. So no matter what, it's always important to keep thinking about health insurance, and to remain informed.

Unfortunately, there are lots of people who think that nothing bad will ever happen to them. Imagining yourself as the victim of a horrible accident or a deadly disease is not pleasant. As a result, many people exist in a state of denial, not thinking about health insurance because they don't want to imagine themselves in a state where they might really need it. The result? If they do experience a serious medical problem, they're forced to deal with an onslaught of confusing, frightening payment issues at a time when they're in no position to focus and make rational decisions.

The following sections of this chapter will help you make sense of the brave new world of health insurance so you can understand how to get the right type of coverage for you and your family. And once you get your health insurance in place, you'll rest easier knowing that you're prepared for any minor or major medical problem that might come your way.

Where Do You Get Health Insurance?

Most people get insurance through their employers. Most companies in the United States offer some type of health care plan for their employees, whether they pay all of the premium for you or ask you to chip in. So one of the most important things you need to find out about when you accept a new job is what type of health insurance your new employer offers. Often, you're stuck with options that someone else has chosen for you (most likely the human resources department). More and more, though, your employer may offer you several choices. At that point, you have some investigating to do. By the time you're done with this chapter, you'll know how to choose the best option for yourself.

But what if you're self-employed, or your employer doesn't offer insurance? Then you're stuck paying the whole premium yourself, and it's even more important for you to carefully explore your options. You can purchase insurance directly from either an insurance company or an HMO that offers individual plans, but that's the most expensive avenue for you. Your best bet is to try to find an organization or association to join that will offer you group medical benefits. Contact the alumni association of the college you went to, or join a trade association that represents people in your professional field. They often offer group medical insurance. Some religious organizations also offer insurance.

ACCIDENT AND SINGLE DISEASE INSURANCE— DON'T DO IT

You've seen the ads in tabloid newspapers. They tout insurance to pay for your bills if you have a specific disease such as cancer. Other policies may pay a specific amount of money if you lose an eye or a leg. Don't buy these types of insurance.

Your comprehensive insurance policy or your managed care program will pay for most of the bills associated with a serious illness or injury from an accident. It costs a lot just to pay for the standard insurance you need. Why buy additional coverage you don't need?

The Four Basic Types

There are four basic types of health insurance. The one you choose will be determined by your needs, what is available to you, and what you can afford to pay.

The four are:

- Fee-for-Service Plans

- Health Maintenance Organizations (HMOs)

- Preferred Provider Organizations (PPOs)

- Point-of-Service Plans (POSs)

Several factors distinguish these types of plans from each other, including: how you pay your premiums and to whom; when you pay premiums; how and when you file claims; how much coverage you can obtain; where you can go for your medical needs; what services are covered.

Be forewarned. You'll never get a policy that pays for everything. Deciding what's best for you involves making some tradeoffs. Of course, the better you understand your options, the more control you will have over making those trade-offs. Take the time to compare policies carefully to make sure you're getting the most from the plan you choose.

Fee-for-Service Plans

Typically the most expensive kind of health insurance, fee-for-service or indemnity plans, are traditional insurance plans that involve paying a monthly premium in return for health insurance coverage. Each time you visit the doctor or stay in a hospital, you get a bill. You then submit this bill to your health insurance company, which will in turn pay your doctor. (The physician or hospital will sometimes directly submit your claim for you, sparing you the trouble of filing all those forms.)

Sometimes you will need to pay the doctor up front. In that case, rather than receiving the bill, you'll receive a receipt which you'll need to send to your insurance com-

pany, again with the appropriate form. Then you'll have to wait, sometimes as long as 60 days, for your reimbursement to arrive in the mail.

Fee-for-service plans consist of three components:

1. Doctor visits

2. Hospital/surgical

3. Major medical

Although once upon a time these three parts were separate and distinct entities, today they are usually combined into one package called comprehensive insurance.

Deductibles and Out-of-Pockets

No matter which component of fee-for-service plans you deal with, there are two key elements: the deductible and the out-of-pocket maximum amounts you are expected to pay. The higher your deductible and your out-of-pocket maximums, the lower your premiums will be. Here's how it all works:

- *The annual deductible.* This is the amount of your medical bills you are expected to pay out of your own pocket before your medical coverage kicks in. Deductibles typically range from $250 to $2,500. For example, if your deductible is $250, you will be expected to pay out of your own pocket the first $250 of medical bills you incur in a year. You will still need to file those bills with the insurance company so they can keep track of how much you've spent and know when it's time for them to

REJECTED BUT FLUSH

If you have been turned down for health insurance coverage because of a medical condition or disability, but you have the big bucks to afford private insurance, contact your state insurance department. Many states have arranged for a private policy you can purchase. Various state plans cover such serious health problems and existing medical conditions as: heart disease, cancer, diabetes, liver or kidney diseases, lupus, AIDS, chemical dependency, mental illness, cystic fibrosis, cerebral palsy, hemophilia, and muscular dystrophy. You may have to pay a bundle for the insurance, and keep in mind that some states limit the total number of applications that they will accept per year, based on their budgets to cover high-risk cases.

Does Your Insurance Cover Birth Control?

Probably not. When Jill Wallace discovered that her health plan would not pay for preventive birth control, she decided to do a little research. She found that although half of the health plans in this country cover at least one method of birth control, only 15 percent of the plans cover all the major methods.

This may be changing, though. The U.S. Senate is considering the Equity in Prescription Insurance and Contraceptive Coverage Act, which could force health insurance prescription drug plans to extend benefits for FDA-approved prescription contraceptive drugs or devices and require plans that provide benefits for outpatient health care service to include coverage for visits to discuss the use of contraceptive devices. In the meantime, although you may be covered for the morning-after pill and procedures like abortion and sterilization, contraception is most likely your financial responsibility.

begin kicking in some funds. Raise the level of your deductible and you can cut the cost of your premium.

- *The coinsurance provision.* Coinsurance refers to those portions of the medical bills for which you are responsible. Typically, a fee-for-service policy requires that you pay 20 percent of your medical costs up to a specified amount (your out-of-pocket maximum, sometimes called a "stop loss"). This type of coverage is referred to as 80/20 coverage. For example, if you have a $500 deductible and a $3,000 maximum out-of-pocket (as defined below), you will be expected to pay the first $500 of your medical bills outright. After that, you'll have to pay for 20 percent of your medical bills while the insurance company pays out the other 80 percent. Once you've paid $3,000 of your own money, however, the insurance company will pick up 100 percent of your bills until the end of the year, when it starts all over again.

- *The out-of-pocket maximum.* That 20 percent copayment portion of the bills can add up quickly to a huge amount. Fortunately, most policies specify that after you have paid out a certain amount of money—your out-of pocket expenses—during a calendar year, you will no longer have to pay the coinsurance fees. Thus, once you've forked over a certain maximum level of dollars, your policy pays for all the costs.

HEALTH INSURANCE FOR KIDS

One nine-year-old Massachusetts boy's middle-class parents could not afford health insurance for him until they discovered a state-operated low-cost health insurance for kids only. Although access to health coverage has traditionally been out of reach for low-income people, recently middle-class families have also been excluded from protection, as spiraling costs force employers to limit coverage to employees only—leaving their families out in the cold. Other states that offer kids-only health insurance plans include Florida, New York, Pennsylvania, and Tennessee.

A Little More Lingo

Hang in there. We're almost finished with definitions. Here are three more to add to your insurance vocabulary:

1. *"Usual, customary, and reasonable costs."* Whether your policy pays for medical services in full or only a specified amount for an individual service, the reimbursement amount is based on the "usual, customary, and reasonable" (UCR) costs for a procedure in your area. For instance, your doctor might charge $85 for an x-ray, but the policy may pay for only $65 if the usual, customary, and reasonable cost charged by medical providers in your area is deemed to be $65. You'll be responsible for the remaining $20 even if you've reached your out-of-pocket maximum for the year. If you haven't reached your maximum, you'll also have to pay the 20 percent copayment.

2. *Lifetime aggregate.* Most policies put a cap on the amount of money they will pay in medical costs over your lifetime. It's important to know what that cap is because it can certainly come into play if you have a catastrophic illness that requires extensive medical treatment. Lifetime maximums typically run from $1 million to $3 million. A few companies offer no lifetime maximum limits. If one of these companies also provides the benefits and services you need with a premium you can comfortably afford, consider signing on.

3. *Services covered.* Always read your policy carefully to see what kinds of services it covers. In particular, coverage can vary greatly with regard to prenatal care, mental health, prescription drugs, and catastrophic illnesses. Moreover, certain procedures, treatments, and drug therapies, such as artificial insemination and some experimental cancer treatments and drugs, may not be covered at all.

Anatomy of Fee-for-Service Plans

Here's a dissection of the different parts of fee-for-service plans. Many fee-for-service plans cover only those visits to doctors for treatment of illness rather than annual

physicals or other visits for prevention of illness. In addition, unlike many HMOs and PPOs, most fee-for-service plans do not pay for services like gym memberships, chiropractic care, and wellness programs. A fee-for-service plan, however, gives you the most freedom to choose doctors. You don't have to worry about which doctors are or aren't covered under your plan, because as long as the medical service you're seeking is covered, you will be reimbursed no matter which physician you see. Doctor visits are subject to both deductibles and copayments.

Hospital/surgical insurance provides benefits for medical conditions requiring hospitalization that are covered by the policy. This type of insurance doesn't cover anything out of the hospital. Normally, these benefits include your room, meals, surgery, physicians, nonsurgical services performed in the hospital, outpatient diagnostic x-rays and laboratory tests, and other hospital services.

The benefits for hospital room and board may be covered for a daily dollar amount or, as is becoming more common, in terms of the hospital's daily rate for a semiprivate room. The policy specifies the types of surgical procedures covered. If a procedure is not covered—like most cosmetic surgery—you can't get reimbursed.

Some hospital/surgical policies, sometimes called "basic" policies, provide "first dollar coverage." This means you don't pay a deductible. Other policies call for a small deductible. Thus, although

ADVOCATING FOR ALTERNATIVE TREATMENT COVERAGE

When Margaret discovered her employer-sponsored health plan didn't cover home births, she decided to try to change the policy. Alternative health care advisers warn consumers that sometimes these therapies aren't covered because insurance companies don't perceive a demand, so Margaret's first step was to let the insurer and the benefits people at her company know about her plans to use home birth. The next step was an education process for the health care administrators. She asked a local midwifery practice to write a letter to the company benefits manager detailing the care patients receive, including statistics that indicated the cost-effectiveness and success of home births. The benefits manager forwarded the letter to the insurance company, and to Margaret's pleasant surprise, her efforts convinced the insurer to change the coverage to include home birth.

your out-of-pocket expenses may be low for a short-term hospital stay or routine surgery, lengthy hospitalization and costly medical care are usually not covered at all by this part of your policy.

Major medical makes up the difference when your hospital/surgical insurance falls short. It pays for costs from serious illnesses both in and out of the hospital. Although there are variations, these policies generally pay most hospital expenses in full or at a rate of 80 percent of the bill.

HANDING OVER YOUR RECORDS

When you apply for some kinds of insurance—especially life and health—the insurance company may want to see your medical records. It's one way insurers assess whether you are a good risk. You will be asked for your consent, but if you decline, the company has the right to deny you coverage.

What Do Fee-for-Service Plans Cost?

With a fee-for-service plan, you'll be required to pay an annual deductible before the insurer pays anything. Deductibles typically range from $250 to $2,500. The higher the deductible, the lower your premium. After you've met your deductible, you pay a coinsurance amount of the balance ranging anywhere from 20 to 50 percent, although 20 percent is most common. The insurer picks up the rest. In addition, most policies specify a yearly out-of-pocket maximum. The lifetime aggregate that the insurer will pay during the lifetime of your policy is usually capped at $1 million.

Premiums for individual health insurance are based on a variety of factors including your age and gender, where you live, whether or not you smoke, and what kind of general health you are in when you sign up. Keeping these factors in mind, plus the fact that the amount of the deductible can severely change the premium, take a look at this example. Jane, a 33-year-old non-smoker with a $250 deductible and a policy that includes maternity benefits, can expect to pay a yearly premium of about $4,000. But Frank, a 30-year-old nonsmoker with a $2,500 deductible, will probably pay a yearly premium of around $500.

Fee-for-service plans were more practical years ago when health care was very different than it is today. In decades past, fee-for-service plans were a lot less expensive, but more limited in some ways. These days, advances in medical technology make available a huge array of diagnostic tests and techniques that did not exist a generation or two ago. Then, the family doctor treated minor, common illnesses, but major diseases often went undetected until it was too late to reverse or effectively treat them. As diagnostic techniques have improved, the emphasis of health care has shifted to early detection and to wellness programs. Unfortunately, fee-for-service plans have not kept up with the times—they still concentrate on covering treatment rather than preventing and diagnosing illness.

When you evaluate a fee-for-service plan, make sure you understand which component covers what type of medical treatments you and your family may need. Some employer-sponsored plans and most plans you purchase on your own let you pick which services you may need. For instance, if you are a single, post-menopausal woman, you do not need the prenatal and pregnancy coverage. Fee-for-service plans are expensive, so buy only the coverage you need.

The downsides to fee-for-service plans are the high premiums and the inconvenience of paying up front, filling out forms, keeping track of your claims, and waiting for reimbursement. In addition there is the troubling aspect of the absence of coverage for preventive medical services. On the other hand, these plans give you the largest degree of freedom when it comes to choosing your own physicians. In addition, with the emphasis on treatment rather than prevention, there are fewer obstacles to collecting for medical procedures or hospital stays as compared with HMOs or PPOs.

Some of the largest companies that sell fee-for-service plans nationwide are:

- Aetna, 151 Farmington Ave., Hartford, CT 06156, (800) 872-3862

- Blue Cross and Blue Shield Association, 225 North Michigan Ave., Chicago, IL 60601, (312) 297-6000

- Mutual of Omaha Insurance, Mutual of Omaha Plaza, Omaha, NE 68175, (800) 775-6000

You can find others by contacting your state department of insurance and asking which are the largest fee-for-service or indemnity plan insurers in your area.

Health Maintenance Organizations (HMOs)

HMOs are less expensive and much simpler to understand than the fee-for-service plans. They also pay for preventive medicine such as baby wellness programs and annual checkups. That's the good news. The bad news is that you give up the freedom to choose the doctor or hospital you want, and you may have to jump through a lot of bureaucratic hoops once you are covered in order to get the medical care you want.

The two biggest differences you'll discover between an HMO and a fee-for-service plan are that you don't have to pay deductibles (except sometimes for prescription drugs) or file insurance claims if you have an HMO. You pay a monthly or quarterly fee instead. Whether or not you use any medical services, the fee remains the same. Each time you go to the doctor, you'll simply have to flash your handy HMO ID card and pay a very modest fee for specific services (called a copay). Typical fees, for example, are $9 for each visit to the doctor or $5 for every prescription you have filled in the managed-care plan pharmacy. These fees are determined by the amount of premium you pay and vary from HMO to HMO. That's all there is to it. No forms. No deductibles. No hassles.

Thus, with an HMO, you may find you have little if any out-of-pocket expenses as long as you use doctors or hospitals that are part of your HMO network. Moreover, most HMOs do not put a cap on your lifetime maximum payments.

HMOs often operate in a group setting. That means that you go to a particular location where the HMO has its facilities and see the doctors and nurses who work for the HMO. Of course, those doctors can and may refer you to an outside specialist or facility if the HMO physicians feel you need such services. In this case, your HMO will pay for those services.

The important thing to remember is that the choice of who takes care of you and what services will be performed is made by the HMO and its physicians, not by you. When you join an HMO, you're usually asked to select a "primary care physician" from the company's list of participating doctors. You are then expected to see that physician whenever you are in need of medical care. That physician will either treat you or refer you to a specialist if you need one. But no matter what, you must start with your primary care physician. That can sometimes be frustrating because it may delay your receiving the care you need. With an HMO, you are trading flexibility and control for lower costs. But you're also trading one kind of red tape for another. You no longer have all those forms to fill out, but there are limitations on the kinds of care you can receive. Because the doctors work for a profit-minded HMO, instead of the patient, they are sometimes restricted to the least expensive type of treatment.

There are 540 HMOs operating in 40 states with total enrollment approaching 60 million. HMO enrollment does vary widely from state to state. For example, in California, over one-third of the population is enrolled in HMOs while in other states total enrollment may consist of only a few thousand individuals.

Taking the Pulse of an HMO

You can reduce the surprises and the disputes you may face by carefully evaluating an HMO. Use this checklist to compare HMOs:

- *In-plan doctors.* Who are the physicians and hospitals in the network? Check to see if the hospitals you prefer using and the doctors you have seen in the past are part of the HMO network.

- *Specialists.* Check out the specialists in the plan. Make sure there are enough of them to choose from and call the American Board of Medical Specialties at (800) 776-CERT to find out if they are board certified. Before signing up for any plan, make sure that you will be allowed to see any of the specialists in the plan and that you won't be confined to only one or two medical groups.

- *Emergency medical services.* Most HMOs do not cover unauthorized treatment in nonmember hospitals. They will pay if there is an emergency. Of course, what you think of as an emergency and what the HMO defines as an emergency can differ. If you go to an emergency room because you

have pains in your chest, but the diagnosis is merely indigestion, your HMO may not pay that emergency bill. In some states—17 so far—emergency treatment must be paid by the HMO no matter what hospital you go to as long as a "prudent person" would have thought that a real health danger existed.

- *Experimental procedures.* Some HMOs voluntarily pay for bone marrow transplants for women with advanced breast cancer, as well as other experimental procedures approved by the FDA. Many more do not. A few states, though, have passed laws requiring HMOs to pay for these procedures. If your state does not require such payment, carefully check the HMO concerning coverage.

- *Mastectomies.* Hard to believe, but some HMOs don't cover even one overnight stay if you have a mastectomy. Fortunately, a handful of states are readying to put laws on the books that would allow a woman to stay in the hospital at least for one night after the procedure. Check out the situation in your state and what your HMO allows.

- *Childhood immunization rates.* This rate is the percentage of young children in the plan who have received their necessary immunizations. The national average is 73 percent. If the HMO's rate is any lower than that, beware. This may mean that the HMO is overloading the physicians so severely that they don't have the time for dispensing routine immunizations. Or it might mean the waiting period to schedule such shots is extremely long.

- *Wait time.* The average time you will wait for a routine appointment with an HMO physician is five to six days from the time you call to the actual appointment. Ask any HMO you're planning to join how much time the patients they cover typically have to wait. Better yet, call one of the primary care physicians in the plan and ask for an appointment. If the appointment they give you is more than six days away, you might want to look elsewhere.

- *Turnover rates.* This rate indicates how many physicians and health care providers leave the HMO network. Here you want to see low numbers.

High rates suggest you may be seeing a different doctor every time you visit the HMO facility because your old one has left. Look for a rate below 10 percent.

- *Percentage of board-certified physicians in the system.* The American Academy of Physicians is the group that confers certification, and physicians must do extensive study and pass a rigorous regimen of tests to gain this certification. Thus, the higher the percentage of board-certified doctors, the better the chances are that the HMO uses extremely well-qualified physicians.

- *Medical loss ratio.* This statistic measures the amount of money the HMO spends on actually providing patient services. You want an HMO that spends as much as possible on medical services. A medical loss ratio of 95.7 percent means the HMO spends 95.7 percent of the money it takes in on medical costs. Only 4.3 percent goes for administrative costs and for profits to those who own the HMO.

- *How the HMO physicians are paid.* Some HMO doctors receive a salary. Others get paid a fee for each service they perform. Beware, though, of plans in which the physician receives a fixed yearly fee for each patient seen. All your medical costs come out of that fee. What's left over goes into the physician's pocket. That's okay as long as there is money left over. But what if your medical condition costs more than what the doctor receives from the HMO? Will you get skimpier services? Probably not, but you don't want to take that chance.

- *The NCQA rating.* The National Committee for Quality Assurance rates HMOs on a number of factors such as the credentials of the physicians, subscriber turnover, complaints, and the like. The NCQA has not completed its rating for all HMOs. If yours hasn't been rated, it doesn't mean there is anything wrong with it. But if your HMO gets low marks, you should seriously consider finding another alternative. You can get a list of the NCQA ratings in two ways: by phone at (800) 839-6487, or on the Internet (http://www.ncqa.org).

Are HMOs Better than Traditional Fee-for-Service Plans?

If you've ever seen a medical show on TV, with heroic doctors sparing no expense to save the patient, you know about popular culture's view of health care. We believe medical care is a right, and that there are no gray areas. Fifteen or 20 years ago, you would never hear a television doctor say, "But you're not covered for that."

Were the old days of health insurance really so great? Well, from the point of view of doctors and patients, it was an endless well of money, technology, and benefits, at the expense of the corporations that ended up footing the bill. There's a huge moral hazard associated with traditional medical insurance. It was the doctors who benefited from the payments, and it was the doctors who decided what payments got made.

Most doctors were probably ethical about this special responsibility, but that's irrelevant. With no checks and balances, it was inevitable that hospitals bought ever more expensive machines, doctors ordered ever more elaborate tests, and hospital stays got longer and more costly. With no one really watching the bills, the idea of health care at any price spiraled out of control.

Today, in the era of HMOs and high consumer premiums and long waits for what can seem like indifferent care, many of us long for the good old days. But like all free rides, those days are over, and the intelligent health insurance company is looking at how to work today's system, rather than reverting to yesterday's.

Instead, we've moved to managed care. Doctors have lost some, but not all, of the responsibility for deciding what should be paid for and what shouldn't. More importantly, many doctors are now employees of a company that makes money when you're well and loses money when you're sick.

The dynamic of a health maintenance organization makes sense in principle, though in practice there are still a number of kinks. By applying actuarial and medical thinking across vast populations, HMOs are trying to figure out the least expensive way to keep people healthy.

For example, if a flu shot costs $2 to administer and it keeps 1 out of 50 people from getting the flu (which costs $300 to treat), the smart HMO will proactively give every one of its members a flu shot.

Sometimes, of course, this math gets in the way of individual needs. If a two-day hospital stay for knee surgery would save you from an infection, you don't care very much that on average, one day is more efficient for most people. You're you. Not the average.

The Country's Largest HMOs

HMOs operate on a local or regional level, but many also are a part of a national network. Here are some of the largest HMOs in the country. To locate some of the largest in your area, contact your state department of insurance.

- Aetna US Healthcare, 151 Farmington Ave., Hartford, CT 06156, (860) 273-0123

- Cigna HealthCare, 900 Cottage Grove Rd., Hartford, CT 06152, (860) 726-6000

- Humana, 500 West Main St., Louisville, KY 40202, (800) Humana-0

- Kaiser Permanente, One Kaiser Plaza, Oakland, CA 94612, (510) 271-5910

Preferred Provider Organizations (PPOs)

PPOs are networks of physicians and hospitals who charge on a fee-for-service basis. You can use physicians and hospitals within the network, or you can go outside the network. The catch is that you pay less for the fee-for-service when you stay inside the network than when you go to a doctor of your choice who is not part of the PPO. The point is to encourage you to use the doctors who subscribe to the plan.

Whether inside or outside the network, you will pay deductibles and coinsurance. When it comes to copayments inside the network, you may either pay a straight fee per office visit—$10 is standard—or you may have to pay 10 to 20 percent of the billed charges. Go outside the network, and that copayment can rise to 30 percent. Your out-of-pocket caps also vary. Unlike HMOs, they do carry a lifetime payout maximum—typically $1 million to $2 million.

A PPO is a good deal if you stay within the network. So, you ask, does that mean my first choice should always be a PPO? Not necessarily. Many PPO networks are small. They may not have the wide choice of in-network physicians you think you may need, although in general, PPOs with smaller networks have lower premiums. If you go outside the network, the lower cost of the annual premium can quickly be eaten up by the higher cost of the deductibles and copayments. Remember, health insurance is a game of trade-offs.

PPOs offer a form of health insurance that costs less than fee-for-service plans but more than HMOs. The big disadvantage of PPOs is their limited scope. They may not offer a full range of specialists, or they may offer just a very few physicians from which you can choose. For example, if you are plagued with lifelong back problems, check to see that the PPO you are considering has an ample number of specialists—board-certified is the key—who can treat your ailments. If not, you may find you need to go outside the system to get the necessary medical care, and that will be more costly for you.

Some examples of PPOs are:

- Blue Cross and Blue Shield Association, 225 North Michigan Ave., Chicago, IL 60601, (312) 297-6000

- DirectCare America, 4301 Darrow Rd., Stow, OH 44224, (330) 686-7030

- SelectSource℠, Cigna HealthCare, 900 Cottage Grove Rd., Hartford, CT 06152, (860) 726-6000

Since many PPOs operate on a regional level, you can find others by contacting your state department of insurance.

Point-of-Service Plans (POSs)

A POS plan combines features of an HMO and a PPO. Here's how it works. If you go to a doctor or facility within the POS network, the plan works like an HMO. Thus,

you pay a small fee for each doctor visit or prescription. You don't have to pay deductibles, and there is no out-of-pocket or lifetime maximum payments. When you go outside the POS network, the plan acts like a PPO with deductibles and co-payments.

POSs have the advantage of allowing you in some instances to use HMO–style doctors and hospitals—and thus pay no deductible and very low fees—and letting you go to the physician you want for other specific services. Thus, you might opt to pay the additional fee to see the gynecologist of your choice for a diagnosis, but to use the POS network should you need to enter the hospital to have a hysterectomy.

Like PPOs, POS plans also tend to be small in terms of the number of physicians and hospitals in the plan. A POS, though, is a good choice if you are wedded to a physician who is part of a POS plan. Because they operate mainly on a regional level, a good way to find one is to contact your state department of insurance for a list of the largest ones in your area.

Medical Savings Accounts

Medical Savings Account (MSAs) plans are one of the hottest topics on the health insurance front these days, thanks to the Health Insurance Portability and Accountability Act of 1996 (HIPAA), which established them. But what exactly is an MSA?

An MSA plan is essentially a health plan with an investment component. It allows you to make tax-deductible contributions to an account out of which you then pay for your health coverage.

An MSA plan is similar to a fee-for-service plan in that it involves premiums and deductibles and allows you to see the doctors of your choice. The difference, however, is that an MSA plan has a lower premium and a higher deductible. In fact, the premiums are even lower than HMO, PPO, or POS premiums. Here's how MSAs work.

You begin by selecting a fee-for-service plan offered by your insurer. In order to turn your plan into an MSA plan, you have to choose a deductible that is at least $1,500 and no more than $2,250. If you are insuring your whole family, the deductible must

be at least $3,000 and no more than $4,500. These deductibles are mandated by the HIPAA. Then the insurance company determines your premium (which is going to be much lower than under a traditional fee-for-service plan) and sets up your savings account—the MSA.

Ideally, you will take whatever funds you save because of the lower premiums and deposit them into the MSA. Contributions to your MSA are tax-deductible. When you need health care, you withdraw money from your MSA to cover it—until you have reached your deductible, of course. The deductible for an MSA plan is much higher than it is in a traditional fee-for-service plan. Once you have paid the full deductible, the insurance company steps in to pay for the rest.

If you and your family are healthy during a given year, there's a good chance that you will have some money left over in your MSA. In that case, you can withdraw that money, but you will be heavily taxed if you do. The point is for you to leave it in the MSA to earn tax-free interest. That way, you build up a savings pool to cover future health care costs.

Right now, to be eligible to set up an MSA plan, you must be self-employed, or you must work for a company that offers MSA plans (the only companies allowed to offer them are those with 50 or fewer employees). If you're self-employed, then you purchase an MSA plan from an insurance company and are responsible for making your own deposits into your account. If you work for a small employer, then your employer will contribute money toward your premium and/or directly into your MSA.

Since MSAs involve tax benefits, some restrictions do apply. First of all, the government has limited the number of total participants in MSA plans to 750,000 in 1997. Also, the Health Insurance Portability and Accountability Act (HIPAA) limits the annual contribution that can be made to an MSA. In any given year, individuals can't contribute more than 65 percent of their deductible amount to their MSA, and families can't contribute more than 75 percent of their deductible amount.

For more information about MSAs you can contact the Council for Affordable Health Insurance, 112 S. West St., Suite 400, Alexandria, VA 22314, (703) 836-6200.

Portability: Cash and Carry

The Health Insurance Portability and Accountability Act of 1996 also provides you with a cash and carry option for your health insurance needs when you're changing jobs and therefore are faced with changes in your health insurance situation. The Act allows you to continue being covered under the insurance plan offered by your previous employer, as long as you pay the premium. You need to be aware, though, that some coverage gaps still exist. If you don't take the right steps, you could find yourself facing huge medical bills with no insurance to pay them.

Under HIPAA, you as a new employee must be covered by your employer's health plan if you had been covered by your previous employer's plan. You can't be refused coverage or charged higher premiums for any pre-existing conditions that were covered by your previous plan. If you become self-employed, the insurers providing your individual coverage must also provide coverage under the same conditions.

Now for the gaps in the coverage. Your new employer doesn't have to extend coverage to you for up to one year. The law only requires that once coverage begins, it can't be discriminatory. Thus, if you weren't covered before by a plan, or your new employer doesn't have a plan, your new employer doesn't have to cover you at all.

So how do you fill that gap? COBRA is the answer for most people who have been part of a group plan covering more than 20 employees. COBRA stands for the Consolidated Omnibus Budget Reconciliation Act of 1985. This law requires employers to continue your medical coverage for up to 18 months after you leave the job—and to offer coverage for your spouse and dependent children for up to 36 months.

Unfortunately, COBRA coverage doesn't come cheap. Typically, you will pay the same group rates your employer does, plus a 2 percent surcharge to cover your employer's administrative expenses. More important, though, you will be covered until your new employer's policy kicks in.

The same rules apply if you become self-employed. You can use COBRA to extend coverage until you find an individual insurance policy. However, to be guaranteed coverage under the new law regardless of your health or pre-existing conditions, you

must have been covered under a group plan for at least 18 months, and you must exhaust your 18 months of COBRA coverage. Only then is an insurance company obliged to cover you.

Warning: You must request COBRA coverage within 60 days of the end of your employment. Your employer is obligated to cover you for up to those 60 days. Fail to request COBRA during this window of opportunity, and you are plain out of luck.

You may find COBRA to be valuable if you are a college graduate. Once you graduate, you often are no longer covered by your parent's policy. COBRA can extend coverage until you qualify under an employer's plan. Unfortunately, if you were covered by the college's medical plan, COBRA doesn't apply. Coverage expires upon graduation. In this case, you should try to buy a short-term bridge health plan until an employer's plan takes effect.

HEALTH insurance for farther down THE ROAD

In the case of insurance, a little knowledge means a lot of security. Take some time now to familiarize yourself with the insurance you'll need later in life.

Right now, you're young and vibrant. At this point, your health care concerns are centered around constructing a floor for your overall insurance plans. Today, that floor consists of the plans your employer offers or those you purchase on your own.

If like millions of other Americans you're in the sandwich generation, then you have to worry about the health care needs of yourself, your children, and your parents. Even if your parents require no financial help from you, they still may need assistance in understanding the host of Medicare rules and regulations. By familiarizing yourself with Medicare, you can make sure that your parents get the most from this govern-

ment benefit. Furthermore, your parents may also need additional health care coverage in the form of private insurance plans called Medigap policies. So, it's time to bring yourself up to speed on the health care programs for the golden years.

Medicare

Welcome to the epitome of bureaucracy. It's called Medicare, and it can drive you to distraction when you try to figure out what is covered, by whom, and for how much. But getting the clues about Medicare isn't as difficult as you might expect. Take a look.

Medicare is the government program of hospital and medical insurance for people age 65 and over. Some disabled people and some with certain serious medical conditions such as permanent kidney failure may also qualify for Medicare even though they're younger than 65.

Don't confuse Medicare with Medicaid. Medicaid is for low-income people. It is also for the elderly who have exhausted all of their assets and need their medical care (such as nursing home care) paid for. Medicare is for the elderly who have the resources to pay the Medicare premiums, deductibles, and coinsurance payments that this government program requires.

Medicare consists of two programs:

1. The Hospital Insurance Plan (Part A), which helps pay for care in a hospital or skilled nursing facility as well as home health and hospice care

2. The Medical Insurance Plan (Part B), which helps pay doctor bills, other outpatient hospital care, and other medical services not covered in Part A

The bureaucratic maze starts with qualifying for and enrolling in Medicare programs A and B. Your first qualifying hurdle is attaining the age of 65. If you have worked 40 quarters and have had FICA deductions from your paycheck for those quarters, you can get the Part A Medicare program without paying any premium. If you have not accumulated the magic 40 quarters, you can buy into the system. You do that by paying a monthly premium of between $187 and $311 for Part A.

To get Medicare Part B, though, you and everyone else must pay a monthly premium of $43.80. You can have this deducted automatically from your Social Security check.

You are automatically enrolled in Part B when you become entitled to Part A, unless you state you don't want it. Even if you decide not to buy into Part A, you generally can still buy Part B (assuming you're 65 years or older).

So that's how you become qualified for Parts A and B. But how do you actually enroll? For those of you who have been receiving Social Security benefits prior to age 65, you're automatically enrolled at age 65. If you haven't been getting such benefits, you will need to contact the Social Security Administration office in your area. Do that three months before you hit age 65. This will give you a time cushion to get the forms sent to you, and then to get the paperwork completed.

Don't procrastinate. You must enroll within four months of your 65th birthday. If you wait more than four months, then you'll have to wait until January 1 of the next year, and at that point you'll only have until March 31 to apply. Moreover, your coverage won't begin until July 1.

Worse still, there are financial penalties for taking your time to enroll. For every year after your 65th birthday that you wait to enroll in Part B, you'll be paying an extra 10 percent in premiums. In other words, if you wait for two years after turning 65 to enroll in Medicare, then you'll always be paying 20 percent more than what you would have paid if you had joined at age 65. If you wait for three years, you'll be paying 30 percent more, and so on. For Part A, though, the penalty for waiting is capped at 10 percent.

What happens if you continue to work beyond age 65 and you're still being covered by your employer-sponsored health care plan? Should you wait to enroll, or not? If you're eligible for the premium-free Part A (and you probably are, since you've probably accumulated 40 quarters if you're still working), then go ahead and enroll in Part A. It won't cost you anything. Furthermore, you'll be able to tap into any Medicare Part A benefits that your employer-sponsored plan does not cover.

Whether you should enroll in Part B (which, remember, costs $43.80 per month) depends on how long after age 65 you expect to work. If it's just a year or two more, it probably makes more sense not to enroll immediately. You will indeed be charged the extra 10 percent 12-month delay fee—but you'll save the $43.80 monthly premium.

For example, if you wait until age 67 to enroll, you will end up paying $53 a month for Part B, but you will have saved over $1,100 in premiums. But don't wait more than five years to enroll. By then you'll be paying almost $78 a month. If you've taken the money you would have used to pay premiums from ages 65 to 70 and socked it away to earn interest, that money will then pay your premiums for another three years. But your premiums will be increasing exponentially, and if you wait another five years until you're 75, you'll be paying $113.60 a month for that $43.80 per month policy!

Now, let's look a little more closely at exactly what Part A and Part B cover.

The Hospital Insurance Plan (Part A)

Part A pays for medically necessary inpatient care in a hospital and a skilled nursing facility after a hospital stay. It also pays for home health and hospice care and 80 percent of the approved cost for wheelchairs, hospital beds, and other durable medical equipment (DME) supplied under the home health care benefit. Coverage is also provided for whole blood or units of packaged cells—after the first three pints—when they are given by a hospital or skilled nursing facility during a covered stay.

Medical hospital and skilled nursing facility benefits are paid on the basis of benefit periods. Here's where Medicare becomes a little tricky. A benefit period begins the first day you receive a Medicare-covered service as an inpatient in a qualified hospital. It ends when you have been out of a hospital or other facility such as skilled nursing home or rehabilitation center for 60 days in a row. It also ends if you remain in a facility other than a hospital that mainly provides skilled nursing care or rehab services but you do not require skilled care services for 60 days in a row.

If you go back to the hospital after 60 days, a new benefit period begins. Your hospital and skilled nursing facility benefits are renewed and you must pay another hospital deductible. There is no limit to the number of days or benefit periods you can have for hospital or skilled nursing facility care.

Nuts and Bolts of Inpatient Care

Part A helps to pay for up to 90 days of medically necessary care in a Medicare-certified hospital in a benefit period. During the first 60 days, Medicare pays all covered costs

Patient Advocates
to the Rescue

If you ever find yourself up against a brick wall fighting for your health insurance rights, you may want to consider turning to a patient advocate like Jacqueline Fox for help. Fox is a Washington, DC, lawyer who goes to the mat for her clients battling insurance companies. A one time corporate securities attorney, Fox's first client in her new career was her mother, a cancer patient whose insurance company denied her coverage. Her successful challenge led her to begin to champion the causes of other patients who felt they had been wronged.

Many cases end before they reach the hostile stage. Although patient advocates can represent clients in court, other services include interpreting policies, reviewing medical bills, and mediating between patients and insurance companies. Patient advocates charge either annual fees of about $250, which include these services, or hourly rates that range from $25 in rural areas to $100 in major cities.

For information about patient advocates and your rights as a patient contact:

Jacqueline Fox
5746 McArthur Blvd.
Washington, DC 20016
(202) 966-5610

except for the first $760. That's the hospital deductible for 1997. You only pay it once no matter how many times you go to the hospital during the benefit period.

For the 61st through the 90th day of a benefit period, Medicare pays all covered hospital costs except for coinsurance of $190 per day. You are responsible for paying that. That's a lot of copayment, which is why many people purchase Medigap policies (covered later in this chapter) to cover the difference.

In the unlikely event that you are in the hospital for more than 90 days in a benefit period, you can use "reserve days" to help pay the bill. You have a supply of 60 reserve days during your lifetime. When you use a reserve day, Medicare pays all covered costs except for daily coinsurance of $380.

There are some gaps in your Medicare inpatient coverage. Medicare won't pay for:

- A private hospital room, unless medically necessary, or for a private nurse

- Private convenience items such as a telephone or television in a hospital room

- Nonemergency care in a hospital that does not participate in Medicare

- Care received outside the United States and its territories, except under limited circumstances in Canada and Mexico

Medicare Part A also helps pay for up to 190 days of inpatient care during your lifetime in a psychiatric hospital. Inpatient care in a psychiatric hospital is subject to the same terms and conditions as regular inpatient care in a general hospital. If you receive psychiatric care, though, in a general hospital, there is not a limit on the number of days of care you can receive in a lifetime.

Skilled Nursing Care Facility

A skilled nursing facility is different from a nursing home. It is a special kind of facility that primarily furnishes skilled nursing and rehabilitation services. Typical patients in a nursing care facility are stroke victims who need physical and speech therapy, or people who have injured themselves in an accident and now need physical rehabilitation.

Part A helps pay for up to 100 days of skilled care in a skilled care facility during a benefit period. All covered services for the first 20 days of care are fully paid by Medicare. The services for the next 80 days are paid by Medicare except for a daily coinsurance fee of $95, for which you are responsible. You'll have to pay all charges for services starting with day 101. At this point, you will have to choose between paying the bill yourself, checking into a nursing home, or returning home to tap into the home health care benefits (more on home health care later).

Medicare will not pay for your stay in a skilled nursing care facility if the services you receive are primarily personal care or custodial services such as assistance in walking, getting in and out of bed, eating, dressing, bathing, and taking medicine. To qualify for a Medicare-covered skilled nursing facility (SNF), you must:

- Require daily skilled care which, as a practical matter, can only be provided by a skilled nursing facility on an inpatient basis

- Be in the hospital for at least three consecutive days (not counting the day of discharge) before entering a skilled nursing facility

- Be admitted to the skilled nursing facility for the same condition for which you were treated in the hospital

- Generally be admitted to the facility within 30 days of your discharge from the hospital

- Be certified by a medical professional as needing skilled nursing or skilled rehabilitation services on a daily basis

Home Health Care

Medicare Part A pays for the full cost of medically necessary home health care visits by a Medicare-approved home health care agency. The home health agency can be a public or private agency that provides skilled nursing care, physical therapy, speech therapy, and other therapeutic services. Services are provided on an intermittent or part-time basis—not full time—by a visiting nurse or home health aide.

INSURING YOURSELF

If you're not covered by an employer-sponsored health plan, and you're not a member of another organization that gains you access to a group plan, you may be trying to buy individual health insurance. You can begin by calling the three largest insurers in your state. Chances are, one of them will have the plan you need—though probably not at the price you were hoping for. Individual insurance is expensive because it's not cost-effective for the insurance companies.

Insurance companies make money on insurance by spreading the risk. An individual buying health insurance is someone who is almost sure he's going to use it—translation: filing claims and costing the insurance company money. When insurance companies sell group policies, they're counting on the fact that many people in the group won't be filing claims. They don't want to sell insurance to an individual or family that's going to be spending tens of thousands of the insurance company's assets.

To qualify for coverage, you must:

- Need intermittent skilled nursing care, physical therapy, or speech therapy

- Be confined to your home

- Be under a doctor's care

A stay in the hospital is not needed to qualify for the home health benefit. You also do not have to pay a deductible or coinsurance. You do have to pay 20 percent of the approved amount for durable medical equipment such as wheelchairs and hospital beds that are provided under a plan-of-care setup and reviewed periodically by a doctor.

Hospice Care

Medicare pays for hospice care for terminally ill people who choose to receive hospice care rather than regular Medicare benefits. Under Medicare, hospice is primarily a program of care provided in a patient's home by a Medicare-approved hospice. The focus is on care, not cure. Hospice services covered under Part A include:

- Physician services

- Nursing care

- Medical appliances and supplies

- Drugs for pain and symptom relief

- Short-term inpatient care

- Medical social services

- Physical therapy, occupational therapy, and speech/language pathology services

- Dietary and other counseling

There is no deductible for these hospice care benefits. Copayments are, however, required for two benefits:

1. *Prescription drugs for pain and symptom management.* You are charged 5 percent of the reasonable cost, but no more than $5 for each prescription.

2. *Respite care for which you can be charged $5 a day.* You can receive inpatient care for up to five days per stay to provide some time off for the person who regularly provides care in the home.

If you need medical services for a health problem unrelated to the terminal illness, regular Medicare benefits are available. When you use these regular benefits, you are responsible for the Medicare deductible and coinsurance payments.

The Medical Insurance Plan (Part B)

Medicare Part B pays for many medical services and supplies, but the most important coverage is for your doctor's bills. Medically necessary services of a doctor are covered no matter where you receive them—at home, in a doctor's office, in a clinic, in a skilled nursing facility, or in a hospital. Part B also covers:

- Outpatient hospital services

- X-rays and laboratory tests

- Certain ambulance services

- Durable medical equipment used at home

- Services of certain specially qualified practitioners who are not physicians

- Physical and occupational therapy

- Speech and language pathology services

- Partial hospitalization for mental health care

- Mammograms and Pap smears

- Home health care if you do not have Part A

While Part B generally does not cover outpatient prescription drugs, it does cover some anticancer drugs and drugs taken orally. Blood is also covered after you meet the three-pint annual deduction.

When you use Part B benefits, you must pay the first $100 each year of charges approved by Medicare. After you meet that $100 deductible, Part B generally pays 80 percent of the amount of all covered services during the rest of the year. You are responsible for the other 20 percent.

Sometimes, however, your share of the bill is more than 20 percent. If you receive outpatient services at a hospital, you pay 20 percent of whatever the hospital charges are, not 20 percent of an amount approved by Medicare. Besides the deductible and coinsurance payments, you also may have other out-of-pocket expenses if your doctor charges more than Medicare has approved for a specific service. You must pay this excess charge.

Make sure your doctors and medical suppliers accept "assignment" of Medicare claims. The doctor then collects directly from Medicare and bills you for the portion that Medicare does not cover.

When Medicare Isn't Enough

By now, you can see that while Medicare pays for a lot, there are holes in the coverage. You can plug some of these holes in three different ways.

1. Purchase a Medigap policy that pays for some of the amounts that Medicare does not and that pays for certain services not covered by Medicare.

2. Enroll in a managed care program such as an HMO from which you purchase health care services directly for a fixed charge.

Pre-existing Conditions

These two words strike fear into the hearts of health care consumers and set the scene for some of the most bitter health insurance disputes.

A pre-existing condition is an ailment that was treated before a new insurance policy took effect. Often, insurance companies will not issue policies to people with serious pre-existing conditions. Those that agree to issue policies sometimes do so at much higher rates. Other tactics include refusal to cover treatment for the pre-existing condition, or the imposition of a waiting period (usually up to one year) before approval of coverage for treatment.

With the rise of genetic screening, the whole issue is becoming even more complex. If people can find out that they're more likely to develop a health problem like cancer or Huntington's disease, should this qualify as a pre-existing condition? Do insurers have the right to know about the genetic makeup of their policyholders and to raise their rates accordingly?

There are policies that don't restrict coverage or charge higher premiums for pre-existing conditions—so if you have a serious medical condition that might leave you out of the health insurance loop, shop around.

3. Purchase a nursing home or long-term care policy which pays cash amounts for each day of nursing care or home care.

Medigap

One of the most popular hole fillers is a Medigap policy. Medigap policies are private insurance policies, offered by most major health insurance companies. As with virtually every type of insurance, it's paramount to buy Medigap policies while you are still in good health. That means buying a Medigap policy as soon as you enroll in the Medicare program. If you wait until you actually have a stroke, or a broken hip, or prostate surgery, you may find it difficult to get coverage.

So how do you purchase a Medigap policy? Start by contacting your state insurance department for a list of insurance companies that offer Medigap policies in your state.

To make it easier for you to comparison shop for Medigap insurance, all states (except Minnesota, Massachusetts, and Wisconsin) limit the type of policies that can be sold to no more than ten standard plans. The plans have letter designations ranging from "A" through "J" with plan A being the most basic benefit package. Each of the other nine plans includes the basic package plus different combinations of additional benefits. Once you are ready to apply for Medigap, make sure you're clear about which policy you are purchasing. Get a detailed list of the benefits from your insurer.

All Medigap insurers must sell Plan A if they want to sell any other plans. Only two states—Delaware and Vermont—do not permit all other nine plans to be sold. Delaware does not permit the sale of plans C, F, G, and H; while Vermont prohibits the sale of Plans F, G, and I.

The ten standard plans do not apply to residents of Minnesota, Massachusetts, and Wisconsin because these states have alternative Medigap standard plans. If you live in one of these three states, contact your state insurance department about the available Medigap coverage.

The HMO Option

An HMO can also fill Medicare coverage gaps. You may have to pay a fixed monthly premium to the HMO plan and small payments each time you go to a doctor or use other services. The premiums and the copayments vary from plan to plan, and they can be changed every year. You must continue to pay the Part B premium to Medicare, but you do not pay those Medicare deductibles and coinsurance.

Usually there are no additional charges no matter how many times you visit the doctor, are hospitalized, or use other covered services. You get all of the Medicare hospital and medical benefits to which you are entitled.

Before joining an HMO plan, ask whether the plan has a "risk" or a "cost" contract with Medicare. Plans with risk contracts have "lock-in" requirements. This means that you generally are locked into receiving all covered care from doctors, hospitals, and other health care providers who are affiliated with the HMO. If you go outside the plan for services, neither the HMO nor Medicare will pay. You'll be responsible for the entire bill.

Cost plans do not carry those lock-in requirements. You can go either to a health care provider affiliated with the plan or outside those providers for services. If you go outside the plan, Medicare will pay your bills that are covered by Medicare. The HMO is not involved. You will be responsible for Medicare's coinsurance, deductibles, and other charges, just as if you were receiving care under the fee-for-service system. A cost plan may be a good choice for you if you travel frequently, live in another state for part of the year, or want to continue to use a doctor who is not affiliated with a plan.

Nursing Home and Long-Term Care Insurance

There are over 12 million people in the country today who, as a result of chronic illness, are unable to care for themselves and who need to avail themselves of some sort of long-term care. Long-term care is differentiated from acute care, the goal of which is eventual recovery. Long-term care patients have no hope for complete recovery, but are in need of services that can help them perform the activities of daily living. The key words here are maintenance of, as opposed to improvement in, their overall medical condition.

Although 57 percent of those who need long-term care are elderly—victims of stroke, Alzheimer's disease, and heart attacks, for example—injuries and chronic medical conditions can strike people of any age. Round-the-clock skilled nursing facilities are very expensive, costing an average of $100 to $200 a day. So who pays for all that if you need that kind of care? Well, actually you do. Or at least you do until all of your assets are used up—then Medicaid kicks in. So, if you are 75 years old, have $150,000 in assets, and become disabled enough to need a nursing home, then you'll need to exhaust all $150,000 paying for that nursing home. Once your assets are down to around $0, then Medicaid pays for you.

If you're thinking there must be a way to circumvent this catch-22 by passing your assets on to your family, be aware that the laws regulating these transactions are complex. The government looks for evidence of this type of financial finagling and has been known to go after the assets to pay for health care even when they've already been given to someone else. So check with a lawyer before you attempt to do anything that might be considered less than up front.

One way to protect your assets without worrying about lawyers and government regulations is to consider long-term care insurance. According to the National Association of Insurance Commissioners (NAIC), long-term care insurance makes sense for people who have over $20,000 in assets (excluding their primary residence).

What Exactly Is Long-Term Care Insurance?

Long-term care insurance pays for long-term institutional or home care as soon as you need it. It pays fixed daily amounts toward the costs—the premiums and benefits vary depending on how much protection you buy. According to the NAIC, you shouldn't spend more than 7 percent of your annual income on premiums.

Long-term care insurance is expensive, though. A recent survey conducted by *Kiplinger's,* comparing premium costs from the top six players in the long-term care insurance business, reveals that the average premium for long-term health insurance in 1997 is $1,189 for a 60-year-old and is nearly double that for a 70-year-old at $2,315. And, if you are 79, that premium, assuming a 5 percent inflation factor, would be $3,443.

Typical Coverage

Most long-term care policies cover $40 to $300 a day for nursing home care and $20 to $300 a day for home health care for people who are unable to perform the activities of daily living (ADLs). These ADLs are tasks like bathing, dressing, going to the bathroom, eating, and so on. The maximum benefit periods vary from two years to an unlimited time with 100 percent of actual expenses reimbursed (although for home health care, daily benefits sometimes are limited to 50 percent of the nursing home care daily benefits).

Who Needs Long-Term Care?

If your family medical history suggests you'll need such nursing home insurance, delay buying it for as long as possible. Instead, take whatever money you would have paid for the premium and invest it in, for example, the new U.S. Treasury bonds that are indexed for inflation. But like any other insurance, this one is a gamble, too. Most long-term care policies are not available for people over age 79, so if you think you may be a candidate, don't wait that long. Also, most policies exclude pre-existing conditions for six months, so you really can't wait until that illness strikes.

Be advised that to get a long-term policy that pays generously, you'll need to spend $3,000 to $7,000 a year for the premium. Do the math. If at age 65 you start investing $7,000 a year, rather than using it for an insurance premium, then you'll get interest payments that can cover your long-term care—and, after 20 years, you'll have made almost $200,000.

To find insurance companies that offer long-term care coverage, an excellent source is Health Connection, an online searchable database of health care services and providers. Visit this Web site (http://www.health-connect.com/) to get information about insurance companies in your state. As always, check with the rating services to be sure they're financially sound before you call them.

Health Insurance: Your Basic Floor Plan

Health insurance is a fundamental part of any overall insurance plan, whether you choose a traditional fee-for-service plan, an HMO, PPO, POS, or a medical savings

account. As with any other type of insurance, you're not married to any policy or type of policy for life. Pick the one that looks like it will suit your needs best right now, and keep your eyes out for new configurations that may look better as your life changes.

Health insurance is a very dynamic part of the insurance industry right now, and it is likely that variations of these basic policies will emerge as new legislation is passed or the market itself forces change. So stay awake out there and watch for them. Health insurance is the floor to your insurance structure. And just as you change the floors in your house—maybe going from carpeting to finished wood floors to tile from time to time—your health insurance coverage can change, too.

INSURE
your income
in case
you're
DISABLED

Whether you are single or married with kids, an accident or serious illness can mean financial disaster. The floor of your plan—your health insurance— is in place, but what if you can't work? You need to reinforce your floor with disability income insurance.

Could you continue to pay your bills if you were unable to work because of illness or injury? If you were to become disabled, how would your family survive? Do you know how much money would be coming in each month and from what sources?

If you don't know the answers to some of these questions, you probably don't have disability insurance. Even if you do have coverage through your employer, it may not be adequate to take care of you and your family's needs.

Disability insurance isn't just for older folks who become ill and can no longer work. A crippling injury can incapacitate anyone. Richard, for instance, is a 29-year-old pharmaceutical rep who broke both wrists playing pickup basketball with the guys one weekend. His job requires extensive traveling, hauling suitcases, sample cases, and other paraphernalia. The temporary loss of his hands prevented him from being able to feed himself, let alone carry out the responsibilities of his job. Luckily, his disability insurance filled in the gap from his lost income until he healed.

If you're single, disability insurance may be a better bet for you than life insurance. Although you are not supporting anyone else, you don't have anyone to support you should you become disabled. Because you have no dependents, your big risk occurs while you are living, not dead. So if you're living alone—particularly if you're self-employed—disability insurance is really a necessity.

Disability Insurance Provides a Paycheck

Disability income insurance is designed to replace a chunk of your income when illness or injury stands in the way of earning a living. To evaluate disability insurance, look at some of the features:

- The duration of the benefit payments. They can vary from a couple of months to a lifetime of benefits.

- The percentage of your income the plan will replace. The cap—set by state law—is usually 60 to 80 percent of your income, but the typical policy that your employer might offer replaces only 50 to 60 percent of your income.

- How sick or injured you need to be to collect.

Disability insurance is available from three different sources. When assembling a package to fit your needs, you'll want to know who offers what. Here are the sources:

1. *Programs offered by your employer.* These are usually paid by the company you work for.

2. *Social Security disability insurance.* Although Social Security does provide disability insurance, you should not rely on it for your sole source of income in the event of an incapacitating illness or injury. The application

process involves filling out forms that document your diagnosis, inability to work, and treatment from doctors and hospitals. Eligibility varies from case to case and is based on less-than-concrete guidelines and who in the Social Security office interprets them. In addition, Social Security benefits are based on the assumption that you have other resources. Because payments are likely to be insufficient to meet your needs, you should plan to supplement this with private coverage.

3. *Private policies.* These you purchase if you can't get disability payments through your employer or through the government, or if their programs do not provide as much coverage as you need.

How do you find out if you have enough protection? Where do you start?

Are You Covered by a Group Plan?

Your first step is to evaluate the sick leave benefits your employer offers. How many sick days do you have? Many employers let you bank sick days if you don't use all of them in a given year. If you've been with your company for several years and haven't used much sick time, you may have a couple of months stored up. The more sick days you have, the less need you have for a disability policy that begins paying benefits immediately after you become disabled.

Now check how long the disability coverage—which kicks in after you've used up all of your sick time—lasts. Some employers offer only short-term disability insurance, which can cover you for anywhere from a couple of months to a year. Others offer policies that pay you benefits for up to five years. Some very generous—and expensive—policies may provide benefits for life.

The good news about employer-sponsored disability insurance is that your employer probably pays the entire cost of the premium. The bad news is that your benefits are taxable.

Moreover, those taxable benefits may not be adequate for your needs. Disability insurance benefits do not replace your total salary. Most policies replace only 60 to 80 percent of your earned income. For example, let's say your employer offers a

policy that replaces 70 percent of your salary. If you earn $40,000 a year, you would receive 70 percent of that, or $28,000. The gap between your original income and the benefits you collect must come from your personal savings, or else you must lower your overall expenses, or both.

When you get the facts about your employer-offered policy, ask:

- How long do the benefits last?

- How much income does it replace?

- How long must you wait before you start getting the payments? For instance, if your short-term benefits (your sick time and your company's extended sick bank, for example) expire after one month, but your disability payments don't begin until after one year, you've got 11 months of living expenses to replace.

- How disabled do you have to be? If kidney failure and the subsequent dialysis treatments you will need make it impossible for you to perform your current job, will the company merely put you into another lower-paying one rather than pay you disability benefits? Under certain circumstances, companies are allowed to do this. The law is fuzzy, but much depends on the level of disability benefits you would collect. Let's say you'd get 75 percent of your salary in benefits from disability insurance, but your employer offers you a job at 85 percent of your previous salary—a 15 percent salary cut. You may have to take the deal if your disability doesn't prevent you from doing the job offered to you. Of course, your employer cannot slash your salary by half in order to avoid having you collect disability benefits.

- Are the disability benefits lowered if you are eligible for Social Security disability benefits? Some policies do this, some don't. Check it out.

Do remember that any policy offered by your employer expires when you leave the job for a reason unrelated to the disability. Unlike your employer-sponsored medical insurance, disability insurance is not portable.

Helping People Get Back to Work

Ten years ago, insurance companies saw an opportunity for profits from disability policies and concentrated on attracting more customers. As the volume of claims grows, threatening to undermine their earnings, the industry as a whole is working toward getting people off disability insurance and back into the workforce.

Companies—like Hartford Life Insurance, for example—encourage recipients of disability benefits to become rehabilitated whenever possible by interfacing with patients and doctors and arranging for services like exercise programs, counseling, and chiropractic sessions. Hartford also provides assistance in job hunting, retraining, transportation to interviews, and has even paid moving expenses for job relocation.

Taking the process one step further, Hartford recently sponsored a wilderness outing in the Florida Everglades for people with disabilities. The benefits to someone like Lisa Kay Standard—who suffers from a muscular disease that caused her the loss of her first-grade teaching position—included a tremendous boost in self-confidence that gave her the courage to face going back to school to get a secondary-level teaching certification. Incidentally, Hartford will pay for her education. The insurance company is counting on Ms. Standard's master's degree to be the ticket to her re-entry to a less physically demanding teaching job.

THE INSURANCE AGENT IS YOUR FRIEND

It's true. After all this caveat emptor talk, it should be reassuring for you to know that most insurance agents and companies act in an ethical and aboveboard manner. Yes, they're in it for the money, but like any other business, in order to make money, they do have to attract customers and keep them happy. And remember, insurance companies are state-regulated and they are concerned about having complaints lodged against them.

Once you have a handle on how the insurance system works—and now you do!— you can really work on building a partnership with your insurance agent. Use her as a resource, because she's the one with access to the latest facts, figures, and research, and if you share your insurance goals and objectives, she's the one who can locate the best policies to suit your needs.

What about Social Security Disability?

Social Security provides disability payments if you have earned enough quarterly "credits," which means you've worked a certain number of quarters of a year and paid into the Social Security fund through payroll deductions.

The dictionary defines disability as "a physical condition that prevents a person from leading a normal life." But Social Security uses a much stricter definition. Unlike private disability insurance, the government's program only pays you if you cannot do any "substantial" work—defined as earning $500 or more a month—for at least a year. The other way to qualify is to have a condition that is expected to result in your death.

Social Security disability is not intended for a temporary condition. Thus, there is no such thing as a "partial" disability payment from this program. For example, if you have two broken wrists that will be mended within six months, Social Security deems that to be a temporary or "partial" disability and will not pay out.

Your benefits also will not start immediately. You are eligible for benefits after you have been disabled for five months and if the disability is expected to last at least one year. The claims processing, though, can take up to two years. Remember, you are dealing with a government bureaucracy. For example, take a look at how long it takes Jeffrey to get disability benefits.

Jeffrey has a severe heart attack on March 15. On March 29, knowing that he is going to be out of work for at least a year, he files for disability. Jeffrey is very fortunate, and his claim is approved on May 30. Now he must wait. September is the sixth full month that he is disabled, so his benefits begin during that month. Well, not quite. Social Security checks are usually paid on the third of each month after the benefits start. Thus, rather than receiving his first check on September 3, he gets his first payment on October 3 to cover the September benefits.

You can see that any snafu might have delayed payments for months. What if Jeffrey had not realized until September that he would be disabled for a full year? What if Social Security had disputed his claim? Would he have had to hire a lawyer? Probably.

So what does snafu-free Jeffrey receive from Social Security? Suppose Jeffrey, 35, was earning $40,000 as the manager of a retail appliance store. As a single person, he might receive $1,200 a month or $14,400 a year in disability benefits from Social Security. If married with children, he'd probably collect more—$1,800 a month for example. Still, that represents only 54 percent of his previous salary.

Private Disability Insurance

To discover how much disability income you might need and whether private disability insurance is a smart move for you, add up all the benefits you might be eligible for under the government and employer programs. Now determine how much you can count on from your own sources, such as savings. Look at your income after taxes. If the total from the employer and government programs is not close to your income needs, you will want to consider buying a private disability insurance policy.

Here are the aspects of disability insurance you will want to consider when you compare the various policies.

The Insurance Company's Definition of Disability

What do you have to do to prove that you are unable to support yourself? Some policies pay you if you are unable to perform the duties of your profession, while others pay only if it's impossible for you to engage in an income-producing activity at all. Some policies

WHERE TO BUY DISABILITY INSURANCE

When you go shopping for disability insurance, you might want to check out the following insurance companies or contact an insurance agent who sells policies for these companies. These firms write a lot of disability policies for individuals:

MassMutual Life
1295 State St.
Springfield, MA 01111
(413) 788-8411

Northwestern Mutual Life Insurance
720 E. Wisconsin Ave.
Milwaukee, WI 53202
(414) 271-1444

Provident Life and Accident
One Fountain Square
Chattanooga, TN 37402
(423) 755-1011

UNUM Life Insurance Co. of America
2211 Congress St.
Portland, ME 04122
(207) 770-2211

allow for partial coverage once you are able to return to work and if you can only start back part time. Most often you'll only be covered for partial disability if you were totally disabled first.

Residual Benefits

These benefits are gap-fillers and are standard in most policies. If your income is cut because you are only able to do part—but not all—of your job or work, your income gap is filled by residual benefits. In most cases, you don't have to start as totally disabled and then move to partial disablement in order to get these benefits. Residual benefits let you move from full employment before you are disabled to partial employment while you are partially employed but recovering.

Elizabeth is a violin teacher who slipped on the ice and broke her leg while walking her dog. In addition to teaching in a music school, she has some private students who come to her house. After her injury, she could not drive, and was unable to travel to the music school to see her students there, although she was able to continue giving lessons to her private students at home. Based on Elizabeth's partial loss of income, she was able to collect residual benefits.

Presumptive Disability

These are benefits that are contingent upon the type of disability you have rather than your ability to perform your job. If you become blind, or totally lose your hearing, or can no longer speak, you can still receive benefits even if you are able to earn a living in spite of these terrible conditions.

Let's say you're a brilliant trial lawyer. You're in a car accident and sustain a head injury that causes total blindness. After your release from the hospital, your firm takes you back, and because you are such a star, they back you up with the resources you need to continue your work—people to read correspondence and briefs, support personnel to help you and be your eyes. Because your disability is so horrendous, you can collect presumptive disability benefits—even if you're getting the same salary you got before your accident.

Amount of Benefits

The size of your monthly disability check is directly tied to the amount of money you earned by working prior to becoming disabled. But you will not be able to get a policy that replaces 100 percent of your earned income. The most any policy will pay is 80 percent. That's because the insurance companies want to provide an incentive for you to return to work. The cost of your premium is determined by the amount of income the policy is designed to replace. The greater your stable earned income, the more you will pay for a disability policy. The percentage of your income you want to replace will also increase the cost of the premium. A policy that replaces 80 percent of your income will be more expensive than a policy replacing 60 percent.

Starting Date of Benefits

Disability policies offer you a choice as to how soon you can begin collecting benefits after you become disabled. The longer you wait to collect, the lower your premium will be. Thus, the waiting period you choose is akin to a deductible. Opt for a short waiting period—31 days is the shortest—and you will pay more for disability insurance than if you choose a six-month waiting period.

Length of Coverage

Once you've determined how long you want to wait for your payments, then you can determine how long you want those payments to last. The longer you want payments,

the higher the premium will be. Policies are available that pay benefits for one year, two years, five years, to age 65, or for a lifetime. You really only need disability benefits for the length of time you had expected to work. If you are 55 years old and plan to retire at 65, you only need disability payments for the ten years until you retire and Social Security kicks in. Make sure you do not buy more disability insurance than you need.

The earlier you buy disability insurance, the less expensive it is per year. For example, if you're 35 years old and buy a disability insurance policy to cover you until you're 65, it will cost you a lot less per year than if you wait until you're 55 years old to buy the same amount of coverage.

Let's say you earn $40,000 a year and want disability insurance to provide you with a monthly income of $1,000 until you're 65 years old. Here's how much it will cost:

If You Buy the Policy at Age:	Cost per Year ($)
55	1,500
45	1,000
35	700

If you earn $1,000,000 a year and want disability insurance to provide you with a monthly income of $2,000, here's how much it will cost:

If You Buy the Policy at Age:	Cost per Year ($)
55	3,000
45	2,000
35	1,400

The Origin of Your Disability

Make sure any disability insurance you purchase covers both accidents and illness. Some policies pay only for accidents. These are not a good deal, particularly if you are older. As you age, it is more likely that illness rather than an accident will be the cause of your disablement.

Factor Inflation into the Equation

Your disability benefits will remain the same year after year because they are based on the money you earned prior to being disabled. Inflation, though, raises your expenses. To fill the gap, you can get policies that increase your benefits to take inflation into account. Of course, you will pay a higher premium for such inflation protection. You should only consider this option if you are young and looking for a policy that covers you until you retire. Over those 30 to 40 years, inflation can eat up more than half the buying power of the dollars you receive from your benefits. The closer you are to retirement, the less you need to protect yourself from inflation.

Fine-Tuning Your Search

There are a few more aspects of disability insurance that you should consider. These are related to keeping and renewing your disability insurance policy.

Every time you pay your disability insurance premium, you in effect renew your policy. That means that the insurance company can raise your premiums or just decide it does not want to insure you any more. To protect yourself from being left without disability insurance, you may want to consider inserting certain provisions into your basic policy. Take a look at what might work for you.

- *Noncancelable policies* give you the right to renew your policy at the same premium for the same benefits. Your rates won't go up, nor can your benefits be decreased or your policy canceled.

- *Guaranteed renewable policies* let you renew your policy for the same benefits, but your premium for those benefits may cost you more.

- *Conditionally renewable policies* can be canceled by the insurance company in the event of any condition stated in the contract—if you reach a certain age or lose your job, for example. But the company cannot cancel your policy just because you develop health problems.

Go Shopping

Disability income insurance is a very specific niche within the insurance industry. Not all insurance companies offer policies. In years past, the insurance companies targeted well-heeled people in private practice such as doctors and lawyers. But recently, the insurance companies have begun to offer policies that fit the needs of average Americans.

Now you can start comparing policies. No two disability income insurance policies are exactly the same, so unfortunately, you will often be comparing apples and oranges. Make sure you consider the following when choosing a policy:

- Find out how the company defines disability and when you can begin collecting benefits.

- Check to be sure the policy covers both accidents and illness.

- Ask if benefits cover total, partial, and/or residual disabilities or only total disabilities.

- See if the company will pay benefits if you are able to work but suffer loss of hearing, sight, speech, or the use of your limbs.

- Find out what percentage of income the maximum benefits will replace.

- Ask if the policy is noncancelable, guaranteed renewable, or conditionally renewable.

- Determine what the requirements are for length of disability before the premiums are waived.

- Check to see if there is a provision for an option to buy additional coverage without medical insurance at a later date.

- See if the policy adjusts benefits according to inflation.

How Much Will You Pay?

As with most types of insurance, your disability insurance premiums are determined by many factors. The following are eight of the factors that an agent selling you a policy will discuss with you:

• *Occupation.* If you're in a dangerous job, you might very well have trouble getting someone to sell you disability insurance.

• *Level of savings.* The more money you have in savings, the longer the waiting period you can endure. And a longer waiting period yields a lower premium.

• *Earnings.* If you make a lot of money, then the insurance company is going to have to cough up more money if you become disabled. So, the more money you make, the larger your premium.

• *General health.* Someone in good general health is going to pay lower premiums than someone who is already showing signs of potentially becoming disabled.

• *Smoking.* Nonsmokers will pay less than smokers.

• *Age.* Younger folks will pay less than older folks. The assumption is that the older you are, the more likely it is that you will become disabled.

• *Where you live.* Some states have different provisions regulating disability insurance and the payouts associated with them. The state you live in may affect your premium cost.

• *Lifestyle.* If you drink a lot of alcohol or report in sick to work a lot, you're going to pay more for your disability insurance than someone who doesn't.

How Much Is Enough?

When you purchase disability insurance, you can keep your premiums lowest by choosing the longest waiting period. Of course, it's a gamble—but it's not like health insurance, which almost everyone uses at some time. In fact, the real likelihood of your becoming disabled is relatively low, so it's probably unwise to pay a high cost for tremendous amounts of disability insurance. And even though there's a lot of red tape to cut through, Uncle Sam may help you out. If you're going to feel a daily pinch from the premiums you're paying for disability, then you're paying too much.

A Final Word

As with any insurance, you should be sure to check the financial health of the company before you sign on the dotted line. Check the insurance rating companies listed on page 211, and don't go below that "A" standard. Remember, you are relying on the insurance company to be there for you when your income is not.

HOMEOWNER'S *insurance* is for *where you* LIVE

Rest easy. You've got your health and disability insurance policies—the floors of your basic plan—in place. Now you are ready to tackle the construction of the walls for that overall insurance plan.

The walls consist of the property and casualty insurance policies to cover your residence, your belongings, and your car. These policies are made of different elements and involve different concepts than health and disability insurance. That's because

residential insurance covers the home you own, the things in your home, and your legal liability if someone gets hurt on your property or you do damage to someone else or their property.

Of course, the overall concept of insurance is at work here, so you will encounter some familiar terms such as deductibles and premiums. You'll also find some new phrases such as replacement cost, actual cash value, and depreciation. And like other types of insurance, you can buy more coverage as you acquire more things that need protection.

Everyone Lives Someplace

There's a type of residential insurance to cover almost every home—whether you live in a house, condominium, or cooperative you own, or in someplace you rent.

Homeowners in America are better insured than renters, for while 95 percent of homeowners have residential insurance, only 41 percent of renters do. Are home-owners more savvy about insurance than renters? Hardly. The reason homeowners are so well insured is that most mortgage lenders require that you buy some type of resi-dential insurance if you want to get a mortgage. But keep in mind that while renters don't need to insure the dwelling they live in, they may need to insure their posses-sions and protect themselves against the liability of someone being injured in their apartment. We'll group homeowner's and renter's insurance together and call them "residential" insurance.

The Basics

The key to understanding homeowner's insurance is to cut through the jargon and answer the questions: "Just what am I insured for and for how much?" But first, let's look at some of the terms you need to learn.

- *Replacement value* refers to the amount it would cost to replace an insured item today. For example, if you insure your home for the full replacement value and it burns down, the insurance company needs to replace it. Period. So even if you've insured your house for $100,000 but construc-tion costs have risen 25 percent since you purchased your policy, the insur-ance company will need to cough up $125,000 to rebuild your house.

- *Market or cash value* means the amount an insured item is worth on the market today. If you insure your house for market value, you need to periodically reassess this amount and adjust your insurance policy accordingly. The reason is that if your house burns down, the insurance company will give you the amount of cash specified in the policy. Take the house in the previous example. If the $100,000 insurance policy had been a cash value policy instead of a full replacement policy, the owner would only have received a check for $100,000 even though it would cost $125,000 to rebuild.

- *Liability* is the last concept you need to understand before building the residential portion of your insurance structure. Residential insurance covers your legal liability if someone is injured either on or off your property or in your residence. Liability is one of the most important protections you get with residential insurance. If your neighbor slips on your wet kitchen floor and sues you for negligence, or if you accidentally hit someone with a golf ball after a great tee-off, the liability portion of your residential insurance will cover your legal fees and any damages you must pay up to the amount specified in your policy. More on that later.

Replacement versus Cash: Who Needs What?

Although replacement value policies cost up to 15 percent more than cash value policies, they can be worth it for the peace of mind. But if you don't live in the house you're insuring, or if you don't need to rebuild it if it's destroyed, you might want to consider a cash value policy. The reason is that if you purchase replacement value insurance, you must rebuild if something happens that makes your home unlivable. If you have replacement value insurance, when you file a claim the insurance company doesn't hand you money. They pay for your house to be rebuilt. If you have a cash value policy, the insurance company cuts you a check and you decide what to do with the money. You can then rebuild if you want to, but you could use the money to purchase a new house or send your kids to college. Cash value policies work well for people who are insuring second homes, or houses they've bought for investment purposes.

THE LARGEST RESIDENTIAL INSURERS

Bigger sometimes is better, at least when you're shopping for residential insurance. After all, these insurance firms are big precisely because they write so many residential policies. Thus, they are able to spread their risk across a large number of policies— and your particular policy won't seem like a major risk to them. As a result, they'll probably sell you a policy for a lower price than would a small insurance company. Here are some of the best places to start:

- State Farm
- Allstate
- Farmers Insurance
- Travelers Property & Casualty
- CNA
- USAA
- Prudential

How Does Replacement Value Insurance Work?

When you buy a house, the mortgage company may require you to get homeowner's insurance whether you want to or not in order to protect its investment. How do you know how much to get? First, the house gets appraised by both the insurance and mortgage companies. The insurance company will require a minimum of insurance based on this appraised value. It makes sense: If your home is valued at $100,000 and you only buy $50,000 worth of full replacement value insurance, then the company would get stuck paying $100,000 to rebuild, while you were paying premiums for only a $50,000 policy.

The mortgage company will have opinions about your insurance, too. After all, your house is partly (or mostly) their house, depending on the size of the mortgage. As you pay down your mortgage, the bank will own less of your house and therefore require you to carry less insurance. It's a good idea to keep track of that and take advantage of it, if you want to. The danger of reducing the amount of insurance, of course, is that you don't want to be underinsured as the portion of the house you own grows. To figure out how much you need, here's the formula used by many insurance companies:

Multiply the square footage of your house by the square-foot construction cost charged by local contractors. A local contractor should be able to give you an average cost to rebuild your house in the event that it is totally destroyed.

So, how often should you reassess your insurance needs as you pay down your mortgage? During the first five to seven years, most of your mortgage payments will be for the interest on your loan. During this period, although the bank requires you to have adequate insurance, your equity in your home will be relatively small because the bank essentially owns most of your house. As you pay down your mortgage, you should consider reassessing your homeowner's insurance every three to five years. If you suspect construction costs in your area are rising rapidly—which will cause an increase in the cost to replace your house—re-evaluate every three years. If not, every five years is sufficient.

The insurance company determines your premiums by figuring out the appraised value of your house and factoring in inflation and appreciation or depreciation. For example, let's say you purchase a full replacement value policy for $200,000. Two years later, your house burns down. In those couple of years, construction costs have risen by 50 percent. After getting several quotes, the insurance company learns that it's going to cost them $300,000 to rebuild your house. The good news for you is that they have to eat the loss and pay out the $300,000. The bad news is that although your coverage will increase by a certain percentage every year to keep up with rising construction costs due to inflation, your premiums will increase, too. This is the way the insurance company protects its bet. They're gambling that your $200,000 house will not burn down and that they'll collect your premium anyway.

Your policy also involves a deductible. This is the amount of the loss you pay yourself before the insurance company begins to fork over the money. The higher the deductible, the lower the premiums. The standard deductible in a residential policy is $250. Raise that deductible to $500, and you will lower your premium by 5 to 10 percent. Raise it again to $1,000 and you can knock from 15 to 25 percent off the premium bill. One old rule of thumb states: Your homeowner's deductible should be equal to one week's take-home pay.

There are a few other factors that will determine your premium, some of which are beyond your control. Take a look.

- *Location.* If you live in a suburban area, you'll pay less for the same homeowner's coverage than if you live in a city. There is a greater risk of fire and

WHICH IS WORTH MORE—YOUR HOME OR YOUR LAND?

The value of the land on which your home sits is the key to sorting through the difference between replacement value and actual cash or market value.

Replacement value represents the cost to rebuild your home, but not the value of the land it's on.

Actual cash or market value equals what you could sell your home for and, as such, is composed of the cost to rebuild plus the value of the land.

Generally, when a home has increased in value over, say, ten years, the majority of that increase comes from the land appreciating rather than a rise in the cost to rebuild.

The reason the replacement cost does not include any portion of the land value is that if your home were totally destroyed by fire or windstorm, your land would remain.

theft in the city, so the insurance company has to get more premium out of you up front to cover the risk of insuring you if you live there. If you live in a very rural area, however, you'll actually pay more for homeowner's insurance than if you live in the city. The reason is that one of the biggest risks associated with a home is fire. Because it is more difficult to get the fire department to a rural home than to an urban dwelling, you'll probably pay more for that home way out in the country.

- *Materials.* Remember the three little pigs and their houses of straw and wood and brick? Well, it's easier for fire to consume a wooden home than a brick one. Thus, you'll pay more to insure that clapboard house than a masonry one.

- *Age.* Old houses—homes more than nine years old—usually cost more to insure than do new homes. That's because old wiring, plumbing, and roofs make old houses more vulnerable to fires.

Cash Value Policies

To take out a cash value policy, you follow the same steps as for replacement value policies: You determine a value for which you want to insure your house based on its appraisal. For example, if your house is appraised at $200,000, you take out a policy for $200,000. The premiums for cash

value policies are typically lower than replacement value policies because if your house burns down, you get that $200,000—no more, no less, no matter how much it costs to rebuild.

Since property losses are typically only partial losses, property owners are inclined to carry just partial insurance on their property. The "80 percent rule" suggests that you buy a cash value insurance policy for at least 80 percent of the total replacement value of your house. For example, if your house is worth $200,000, buy at least $160,000 worth of coverage. That 80 percent is a critical figure. In fact, insurance companies often won't allow you to purchase any less because if you purchase only $100,000 worth of insurance, legally they could end up having to pay out more, regardless of the actual coverage. They require you, in effect, to become a co-insurer in any loss.

Protecting Your Things

A typical homeowner's policy covers only some of the value of your belongings. Normally, coverage is equal to 50 to 70 percent of the value of the house. For example, if you insure your house for $100,000, your belongings will be insured for $50,000 to $70,000, depending upon your insurance company. You can always add to the coverage for your belongings if you pay a higher premium. So, if you own a lot of valuable things that are worth more than $70,000, you will want to consider increasing your belongings coverage proportionately.

The next step is to decide whether you want a policy that covers actual cash value or one for the replacement value of your belongings. Just as with your house, you'll probably be better off with replacement value, although it does cost a little more.

Typical homeowner's policies cover actual cash value. Unfortunately, you may be in for a big surprise when you file a claim because the payout will probably be significantly less than the cost of replacing the item.

Let's say a windstorm lifts a tree from your front yard, blows it through your living room window, and destroys the sofa you bought five years ago for $2,500. You're not worried, though, because you have homeowner's insurance. But if your belongings are covered for cash value, the insurance company values your five-year-old couch at

GREAT MOMENTS IN INSURANCE HISTORY

Fire insurance gained importance to property owners after the London Fire of 1666. The fire raged for five days, destroying 14,000 buildings and leaving 200,000 homeless. Only a very few of the destroyed buildings were insured. The need for fire protection insurance fueled the creation of a number of fire insurance firms. These firms wrote long-term fire policies on homes and businesses.

whatever it's worth today, or rather, what you could have sold it for just prior to it being damaged. This is called depreciation.

Depreciation is the decrease in the value of something caused by the object's use. After a certain number of years, the thing may have no value according to the insurance company even though it would cost you a considerable amount to replace it.

Look at that $2,500 sofa. The insurance company may say that your sofa had a "useful life" of five years. So each year, it is worth one-fifth (or $500) less than the year before. After three years, the sofa is deemed to be worth only $1,000. They arrived at this value after doing this simple calculation:

$2,500 minus the depreciation (which is $500 times three years or $1,500) equals $1,000. So all you'd get for that couch is $1,000.

However, if your couch were covered by a full replacement policy, the insurance company would have to buy you a new couch that is comparable in value to the couch you lost when it was brand new. Actually, they have a choice. The insurance company can cut you a check, but they also have the right to repair or replace the couch instead. A policy that pays to replace your belongings costs about 10 to 15 percent more than an actual cash value policy. Seriously consider going the replacement cost route. It may save you a lot of money when you have a claim.

Keeping Track of Your Stuff

No matter what type of policy you have, you must keep good records to get compensated for the loss of any contents. This involves two things:

Don't Overinsure

Keep in mind that when you purchase full value replacement cost insurance, your premium is based on the insurance company's appraisal of the value of your house. If you think that their appraisal is too high, you can dispute that. For example, if you purchase a home for $200,000, the insurance company is going to want to sell you $200,000 in homeowner's insurance. The reality is that you've really paid for the house and the property that the house sits on. If the house came along with two acres of property, then you may have actually paid $125,000 for the house and $75,000 for the property. In that case, your house may only cost $125,000 to rebuild and you should only have to pay for a $125,000 replacement cost policy.

If you think you are being asked to pay for more coverage than is necessary to replace your home, check the terms of your mortgage before attempting to dispute it—banks usually require a minimum amount of coverage. If you still believe less insurance will be adequate, point this out to the bank and get it confirmed by an appraiser for the insurance company writing the policy. You have reality on your side. That's because the insurance company will not insure your home for more than it would cost to replace. So get the insurance company to provide the appraisal. If you still are not satisfied, ask two more appraisers to value your home. Ultimately, it is not you or the bank who decides the value of your home. It is an appraiser.

1. Make an inventory of your possessions—either in writing or by taking photographs.

2. Record the value of those possessions. That means keeping the receipts for the things that you want to insure.

There is an inventory list at the end of this chapter that will help you with this task. Set aside one day to go through your home and list everything you might want to insure. Think about what you would need if a fire consumed everything you had. What would you have to replace to restart your life? If you can't set aside a full day, do it in a couple of evenings. Take your inventory room by room. Don't forget what's in the closets, drawers, and under the bed.

Most people tend to procrastinate when they're faced with the chore of making a log of all of their possessions. But keep in mind the basics of insurance that you learned in chapter two:

1. Insurance companies aren't in this business because they are benevolent.

2. Insurance companies are not nonprofit organizations.

3. And if they can find a valid reason not to pay a claim that you filed, they're quite likely not to pay.

For example, say you have a fire in your home and your $3,000 stereo is destroyed. You might file a claim with your insurance company for $3,000. But if you don't have any pictures of the stereo and you threw out the receipt a long time ago, the insurance company has the right to claim that there's no proof that you ever owned such a stereo. They'll write you a $500 check (or some other amount that they deem is reasonable). Without accurate records, you'll have no recourse. Make the effort now to protect yourself later.

Liability

This portion of your residential insurance covers you against lawsuits for bodily injury or property damage that you or your family members cause to other people. It also

Get Guaranteed Replacement Cost Coverage

To get the most protection, seriously consider guaranteed replacement cost coverage. This type of coverage costs, at the most, $10 more annually than straight replacement coverage, but it does have some advantages.

Often, when a disaster hits an entire area—as was the case with the Oakland, California, fire in October 1991—the cost of building materials and labor skyrockets. Local contractors figure—correctly—that most people are willing to pay a little extra to get their houses fixed up sooner rather than later.

In the Oakland fire, a number of homeowners discovered that while they had replacement coverage, the cost to rebuild their homes exceeded their level of insurance because rebuilding costs had zoomed so high for the area.

Guaranteed replacement cost coverage also factors in the general increase in construction prices that occurs as a result of inflation. With this type of policy, you do not have to recalculate periodically how much it would cost to rebuild your house. The policy does that for you.

Tips for Taking Inventory

• Take pictures of each room. You might want to photograph specific items that are valuable. Consider using a video camera for taking inventory. (Don't forget to include the camera in the inventory!)

• List the things in your closets and drawers, and items stuck under the bed or inside linen chests. Make special note of jewelry and expensive gear you might use for skiing or other special occasions.

• List as many specifics about the items as possible. Include serial numbers, the size and make of appliances, and any special features.

• List how much you paid for the item and when you bought it. If you have receipts, attach them to your inventory.

• Update your inventory list every year. Better still, when you purchase something, just add it and the receipt to the inventory list.

• Keep your inventory list in a safe place such as a fireproof container or in a safe deposit box. Your paper list does you no good if it is reduced to ashes in a fire, or if the thief steals the strongbox along with your other possessions.

covers damages caused by your pets to others. Thus, if your dog eats your neighbor's Persian carpet, your residential insurance policy pays up. (If Fido eats your carpet, however, you are out of luck.)

But the big liability you want to protect yourself from is not damage caused by Fido — it's the harm you and your family members do to someone else. Your policy pays for both your legal defense and for any damages a court rules you must pay. Unlike the other aspects of your residential coverage, you pay no deductible with liability insurance. The insurance company pays everything from dollar zero. But there is a maximum amount the insurance company will pay.

If you fall into your neighbor's china cabinet, your residential policy will cover the cost to defend you in court and to pay for the damage to the items in the cabinet, up to the limit of your coverage. Your residential policy also covers liabilities involving injuries to other people who are on your property. Let's say your neighbor trips over that Persian rug and sprains her ankle. Your policy would cover her doctor bills. Again, though, if you trip over your own Persian carpet, your residential policy does not cover that. That injury is covered by your medical insurance.

A typical rule of thumb is that your insurance company will usually require that you carry an amount of liability insurance greater in value than that of your home. The reasoning behind this is that the most expensive thing you own is your house. If someone sues you, you want to be sure you have enough coverage so that if you lose the case, you won't lose your house. For example, if your home is valued at $100,000, the liability built into your residential policy will be some percentage greater than that, depending on the insurer. If your policy covers you for $150,000 in liability and you get sued for more than that and lose the case, you will have to foot everything over that $150,000.

Umbrella Coverage

No, this is not for the damage you might do to your neighbor with your umbrella. It is about coverage above the standard liability level. It's called umbrella coverage, and it is extra liability insurance.

You would need umbrella insurance to pay for that $1 million Incan artifact in your neighbor's china cabinet that you just fell into and completely decimated. Umbrella

CAN YOU BE REFUSED?

Insurance firms, in some states, can refuse to issue you replacement coverage for a variety of reasons. These include:

• You want to insure for less than 80 percent of the replacement value.

• You rent your home to someone else.

• There are more than four families living in your home.

• Your property is particularly vulnerable to theft or damage (for example, if your house was built on swampland and may sink, you may have trouble getting insurance).

• The replacement value of your home is significantly higher than the actual cash or market value.

coverage also takes care of other such legal headaches as libel, slander, defamation of character, and invasion of privacy lawsuits that might be slapped on you.

Remember, umbrella coverage is a totally separate policy, and you buy it as a separate policy. Most people purchase umbrella coverage through the same company as their residential insurance. That's a smart move because you often can get a discount buying from the same insurance company, assuming the basic rates are priced well.

The cost of umbrella coverage depends on the underlying insurance that you have and the amount of liability coverage you want. The less your underlying insurance covers, the more you will have to pay for umbrella coverage.

Take a look at how this works. Let's say you have underlying liability coverage for $100,000. If you want to be protected for a $1 million liability, the $1 million umbrella policy will pay the benefit after you've used up your standard residential liability. For example, if your standard coverage pays the first $100,000, the umbrella pays for the next $900,000. But, if your underlying policy is for $200,000, the umbrella coverage pays for only $800,000 of the $1 million maximum. You won't see the difference in your coverage, but you will see a difference in your premium. The more standard coverage you have, the lower your umbrella premium will be because the umbrella is assuming less risk.

Title Insurance

The bank requires that you buy title insurance when you borrow money from the bank to buy a piece of property. The title insurance makes sure that whoever sells you the property has the legal right to do so. The bank wants to protect its equity in the property while you are paying down the mortgage.

Thus, when you close on a house, you typically must buy title insurance from a title insurance company for about $2.50 for every $1,000 of coverage. The minimum the bank requires is equal to the amount of equity the bank has in your property. That covers the bank's risk.

But what about your financial risk, which is equal to the equity you have in the property? For this, you can purchase owner's title insurance for about $3.50 per $1,000 of coverage. If a flaw in the title comes to light some 20 years after you've bought your home, the title insurance company forks over the money, even if the value of your property has risen ten times.

Since you only buy this insurance one time—when you purchase your property—it can be a very good deal for a lot of protection over a lot of years. On a $120,000 home, you would spend $420 only once for private title insurance that covers your house as long as you own it.

Head 'Em Off at the Pass, Pardner!

Your insurance company may say it wants to protect you, but you need to help them a little. Make sure that the company doesn't have any reason to doubt the legitimacy of your claim. You can do this simply by documenting your ownership of your stuff. Don't stop with the obvious valuables like jewelry and your expensive electronic toys. If a fire wipes out everything you own, the cost of replacing the rest of your belongings—like your clothes, books, lamps, and even the contents of your garage and attic—will be much higher. Be as absolutely thorough and ruthless as you can by taking photos, recording the purchase price and date, keeping receipts, and recording manufacturers and serial numbers. Be sure to include any of the following items you might own.

Objects in main living areas:

- Appliances and fixtures
- Armoires
- Beds
- Bookcases
- Books
- Buffets
- Built-in cabinets
- Carpets/rugs
- CDs/records/tapes
- Cedar chests
- Chairs
- China
- China cabinets
- Clocks
- Clothes
- Clothes dryers
- Coffee tables
- Computers
- Couches
- Desks
- Dishwashers
- Dressers
- Dressing tables
- Electric shavers
- End tables
- Food
- Freezers
- Garbage disposals
- Glassware
- Groceries
- Hair dryers
- Hampers
- Kitchen knives
- Lamps/fixtures
- Linens
- Mirrors
- Musical instruments
- Night tables

- Ovens
- Plants
- Pots
- Radios/stereos
- Refrigerators
- Scales
- Serving bowls
- Sewing machines
- Shower curtains
- Silverware
- Step stools
- Stoves
- Tables
- Televisions
- Toiletries
- Towels
- Trash compactors
- Utensils
- VCRs
- Video games
- Videotapes
- Wall hangings
- Washing machines
- Window treatments

In your garage/basement/attic:

- Automotive tools and supplies
- Bicycle racks
- Bicycles
- Carpentry tools

- Games
- Garden tools and supplies
- Ladders
- Lawn decorations
- Lawn mowers
- Lawn sprinklers
- Luggage
- Luggage racks
- Skateboards
- Skates
- Skis
- Snow blowers
- Snow shovels
- Sports equipment
- Stored furniture
- Toys
- Trash cans
- Wheelbarrows
- Workbench

Outdoor areas:

- Barbecue grills
- Garden hoses
- Mailboxes
- Patio furniture
- Plants
- Storage bins
- Wading pools

HOW DOES YOUR FIRE DEPARTMENT SCORE?

Residential premiums are based on a whole array of factors, some of which have to do with how your house is built and some with where your house is located. For example, fire departments in different towns are rated on the basis of efficiency. If you live in an area that is serviced by a great fire department, it will work to your advantage when the insurance company calculates the cost of your insurance.

On the other hand, the cost of umbrella insurance does increase in tandem with the level of liability coverage. A policy covering $2 million will cost more than a policy for $1 million. Most insurance companies will want you to have a minimum of $300,000 in underlying coverage before they will even sell you a policy for $1 million or more.

The more people in your household and the more property you want to cover, the higher your umbrella coverage will cost. Think about it. If you are single and own one home, you are less likely to be sued than if you are married with six kids and own a home, vacation cottage, and a boat.

Umbrella coverage is another one of those insurance gambles. If you don't own that many assets—and this includes not only your possessions but financial assets such as savings accounts and investments—it may not be worth it to spend the extra money for umbrella coverage. But keep in mind that if you do get sued and lose, your wages can be garnished to pay any settlement. On the other hand, if your total assets are substantial, you definitely want to make sure that these are protected from any lawsuit in which you are found to be financially liable. There are no tried and true rules of thumb regarding whether or not you should have an umbrella policy. In some instances, it's a hard call to make, but if you're concerned about the possibility of losing everything in a lawsuit, the extra money you spend to purchase an umbrella might be worth it for your peace of mind.

THE NUTS
and bolts
of
homeowner's
INSURANCE

Like health insurance that comes in a variety of forms—HMO, PPO, and POS—residential insurance goes by names that are even less sexy. There are six basic homeowner's policies, and they are pretty much the same no matter where you live (except for Texas). These policies tend to be defined by the perils they cover.

THE SINS OF YOUR CHILDREN

When John Miller's 15-year-old son caused $10,000 worth of vandalism damage to a government-owned warehouse building, the state held Miller liable as the parent of the boy—so Miller turned to his homeowner's policy to pay the bill. Although his insurance company contested the claim, Miller took it to court and won.

The court ruled that unless a homeowner's policy specifically excludes coverage for vandalism damage, the insurance company must pay the claim. The court said its ruling protects parents from the possibility of financial ruin and facilitates compensation for victims.

HO-1

This is the basic homeowner's stuff. It covers your dwelling and personal property against losses from 11 types of peril:

- Fire or lightning
- Windstorm or hail
- Explosion
- Riot or civil commotion
- Aircraft
- Vehicles
- Smoke
- Vandalism or malicious mischief
- Theft
- Damage by glass or safety glazing material that is part of a building
- Volcanic eruptions

HO-2

This is the basic homeowner's stuff plus and is thus more expensive than HO-1. It covers your dwelling and personal property against the 11 perils of HO-1 plus six more:

- Falling objects, including trees
- Weight of ice, snow, or sleet
- Electrical surge damages
- Three categories of water-related damage from home utilities or appliances

- Sonic booms

- Damage from water that freezes in the pipes of your heating, plumbing, or sprinkler system

HO-3

This is extended homeowner's stuff. It covers the 17 perils (listed above) unless they're specifically excluded. It also adds coverage for additions you might have made to the structure of your home (like wall-to-wall carpeting) and insures personal property against all perils named in HO-2. Some of the excluded perils are:

- Settling, cracking, shrinking, bulging, or expansion of the foundation

- Insects, vermin, rodents, or domestic animals

- Wear and tear, or aging

- Contamination including but not limited to toxic chemicals and gases

- Vandalism

- Rust or mold

- Flood, earthquake, and nuclear accidents

Seriously consider the HO-3 policy. The coverage is more complete and usually represents a better value. Of course, if you can't afford an HO-3 policy, don't make the mistake of waiting until you can. Opt for whatever you can afford at the time— an HO-1 or an HO-2—and keep the premiums down by raising your deductible.

INSURE YOURSELF

Raising the deductible is one of the easiest and best ways to save on your homeowner's insurance costs. When you do that, you act as your own insurance company. Here's how it works.

Open a savings or money market account and deposit the amount of your deductible ($1,000 for example). Your money will draw some interest, you will pay a smaller premium, and you will have the money to cover the amount the insurance company does not pay if you have to make a claim.

"Insurance firms pay back only 50 to 60 cents on every dollar you give them, so it is always cheaper to set up a self-insurance plan by taking a higher deductible," says J. Robert Hunter, head of the insurance group of the Consumer Federation of America.

HO-4, HO-6

These are renter's and condominium owner's coverage, respectively. Your possessions are covered from the 17 listed perils.

HO-8

This is the basic older home stuff. It covers dwelling and personal property from the 11 perils. It differs from HO-1 because it covers repairs or actual cash values—not rebuilding costs. This is for homes that have some historical or architectural aspects. Thus, the home's replacement cost is significantly higher than the actual cash cost.

What You Get

Now that you understand the perils your insurance policy covers, you need to take a look at the things it covers. We talked about what happens if your home is completely destroyed. That's actually rare. Usually, only a piece of your home is damaged. Your homeowner's policy covers the basic structure and everything in it, including your kitchen, living space, bedrooms, the walls, the roof, and the like.

Most policies also cover structures that are detached from your home. These would include a detached garage or toolshed. The coverage you can get for these detachables is usually limited to 10 percent of the total value of your home. Thus, if you insured your home for $100,000, the garage would be covered for a maximum of $10,000 worth of damage minus the deductible. You can increase the coverage if you have a special need, like a huge garage.

If the garage costs $6,000 to repair and you have a $500 deductible, you would pay $500 and the insurer would pay $5,500. Of course, if the garage costs $11,000 to repair, you would still pay the

INSURANCE FOR LANDLORDS

If a situation exists, there probably is a homeowner's insurance policy to fit it. For instance, if you are a landlord, you can get coverage that insures only the dwelling itself. You have no need to insure the personal property inside the home. That is the responsibility of your tenant.

$500 deductible but the insurance company would only pay $9,500, because only $10,000 of the garage was covered by the policy.

The only way to get full replacement coverage for a structure like your garage is to purchase a rider to your homeowner's policy. However, such a rider rarely makes economic sense, unless the detached structure is worth significantly more than 10 percent of your homeowner's policy.

The Greenery

The trees, plants, and shrubs around your home are typically covered for only 5 percent of the value of the policy of your home. Thus, the most you can collect from a landscaping devastation would be $5,000 on a $100,000 policy. But this varies widely depending upon your company's policy. For example, Allstate imposes a $500 limit per tree, shrub, or plant, and that includes the cost of removing the damaged greenery.

Moreover, the landscaping is usually only covered against fire, lightning, explosions, vandalism, theft, riots, and—hard to believe—falling aircraft. Landscaping is not covered if it is damaged by a windstorm.

Of course, if a tree falls on your roof, your insurance policy covers the repair to the roof and the cost to have the uprooted tree hauled away. Your policy, though, doesn't pay to have that tree removed if it falls on your neighbor's roof. Your neighbor's homeowner's policy covers that, even if it's your tree.

THE TEXAS EXCEPTION

They do things differently in Texas which, after all, was a republic before it was a state. In Texas, there are three basic policies mandated by the Texas State Board of Insurance. These three policies are:

1. HO-A covers your house and its contents against certain perils, but only for their actual cash value.

2. HO-B covers your house and its contents against certain perils. The house is covered for the replacement cost and the contents for actual cash value unless you buy additional coverage to replace the items.

3. HO-C covers your house and contents against all risks that are not specifically excluded. Your house is insured for the replacement value and the contents for actual cash value unless you want to buy additional replacement coverage.

TRY A FAIR PLAN

These insurance programs are known as FAIR plans—for Fair Access to Insurance Requirement plans—and 31 states have them. These plans allow you to purchase some type of homeowner's insurance if you can't get standard coverage from an insurance company. If you live in a state with a FAIR plan, contact your state insurance department about getting covered. Their phone numbers are in the resources section at the back of this book.

Your Belongings

Your possessions are normally covered for up to 70 percent of the value of the insurance on your house. But remember, you can increase that percentage if you are willing to pay extra. It will also cost extra for replacement coverage rather than actual cash value coverage.

Again, there are exceptions and stipulations. Most policies will not cover jewelry, furs, or watches for more than $2,000. Artwork and business items such as computers also are not normally covered. Times do change, however, and more companies are beginning to add computers to the list of belongings that are covered by the standard homeowner's policy. Allstate, for example, covers your computer equipment up to $5,000 on a standard HO-2 policy.

Floods and earthquakes are not covered under typical homeowner's policies either. For these you will need special coverage. To get the scoop on how to insure against these items, turn to chapter ten.

Your homeowner's policy also covers your possessions against theft if you take those possessions out of your home. Thus, if your luggage is stolen from the hotel while you're on vacation in the Bahamas, your insurance company will pay to replace your luggage and the items inside it, not to mention that TV set, stolen from your car on the way home from the repair shop.

Loss of Use

Check to see if your homeowner's policy provides for something called loss of use. Most do. While most people focus on insuring their home or belongings, they forget

how expensive it can be not to have the use of their home. For example, should a fire reduce your house to ashes, where would you stay while it's being repaired? And how much would it cost to stay there?

Most policies will reimburse you for the loss of use of your home to the tune of 20 percent of the insurance on your home. Thus, with a $100,000 policy on your house, you would receive up to $20,000 to pay for short-term rental expenses for another home, apartment, or hotel. You can increase this standard coverage by paying an additional premium.

Shopping for the Best Rate

Would you pay double the price that your neighbor paid for the same pair of khakis? Would you regularly shop at a grocery store that charges twice the price advertised by the competition down the street? Of course not. As a smart consumer, you compare prices and service. Do the same when it comes to buying insurance.

HO-5: HOMEOWNER'S MEGACOVERAGE

Just to see if you were paying attention, we omitted HO-5 from the list of types of homeowner's insurance. Actually, it was left out because although it's the most comprehensive coverage available, it's so monstrously expensive, most insurance companies don't even offer it. While most homeowner's policies cover specifically named perils, HO-5 covers all perils except those specifically excluded (such as acts of war and floods). If you want additional protection, it makes more sense to add supplementary insurance to an HO-3 extended homeowner's policy.

Americans spend over $22 billion a year for homeowner's insurance. Most do not realize that the cost for the same insurance coverage can vary greatly. "Prices for the exact same insurance coverage vary more than 100 percent from one company to another," says J. Robert Hunter, head of the insurance group of the Consumer Federation of America. No surprise then that Hunter recommends that consumers "shop around" for the best rates before they sign on the dotted line.

Cut Your Homeowner's Insurance Bill

In addition to shopping for the best rate for your homeowner's insurance and raising the deductible, there are a number of other ways you can lower the cost:

• *Multiple policies.* If you purchase your homeowner's, umbrella, and auto coverage from the same company, you may be eligible for a 5 to 15 percent discount on your premiums.

• *Add home security.* You can usually get at least a 5 percent discount for installing smoke detectors. Beware of overdoing the security thing, though. Some insurance firms will give up to a 15 to 20 percent discount for sophisticated sprinkler systems and burglar alarms connected to a local police, fire, or private security station. But these systems are not cheap. Compare the cost of installing and maintaining such systems with how much they will save. Often, you may find it's cheaper to raise the level of your coverage than to buy a $1,000 security system. But there are other reasons to install a security system—like safety and peace of mind—reasons that can't be measured in dollars.

• *Stop smoking.* Some companies offer small discounts, but remember everyone in the household must be nonsmokers. Some health insurance policies will cover the cost of quitting; some HMOs even offer a cash bonus if you quit!

• *Home improvements.* If you replace the old electrical wiring in your home or overhaul the plumbing, you may be entitled to a discount because your house has become more fireproof. But if you add a new room, you may have to boost your coverage because that will increase the replacement cost of the entire house.

• *Age has its privileges.* Some companies provide discounts to people who are over 55 years old and retired. Their reason is that retired people stay in their houses more than working people and can thus spot fires more quickly.

When the Going Gets Tough, the Tough Go Shopping

While you may enjoy shopping at the mall for threads and gadgets, you probably don't think of shopping for insurance with the same kind of enthusiasm and sense of fun. But considering the difference in price for the same coverage, it pays to do a little homework. And if you shop for insurance wisely, you'll be able to save enough money to spend more for those goodies at the mall.

To do some comparison shopping, start with a trip to the reference section of your public library. If you cruise the Internet, you can get some great information from the Insurance Information Institute Web site (http://www.iii.org).

Before you even begin looking for price quotes, J. Robert Hunter suggests consulting the two issues of *Consumer Reports* that rate the property and casualty firms with the best service and the cheapest rates. "Many times the companies with the best service also will be the cheapest ones," Hunter observes.

While at the library or surfing the Internet, don't forget to check the financial well-being of your insurance firm. Low rates are meaningless if you can't collect on a claim because your insurance firm has gone belly-up. Eliminate all but the very top-rated firms. A rule of thumb is to go only with firms that sport some type of "A" rating.

YOUR CREDIT CARDS

Good news for you! If you have a standard homeowner's policy, you probably don't need to purchase any separate policy to cover credit card charges if someone steals your credit card and uses it to buy stuff. Most homeowner's policies will pay up to $500 in charges.

So if you are paying an extra $15 or even more through your credit card company or some other organization for credit card insurance, you can stop that insurance and those payments just as soon as you buy a homeowner's insurance policy. Just be sure your homeowner's policy covers that loss.

THE AVERAGE COST OF HOMEOWNER'S INSURANCE

While nationwide the average annual cost for residential insurance is $420, according to a study conducted by the Alliance of American Insurers for the Insurance Information Institute, state-by-state averages vary in a big way—from the high of $548 in Massachusetts to the low of $274 in Wisconsin. Other states with averages over $500, according to the survey, are California, Louisiana, Mississippi, Rhode Island, and Texas. States with averages under $300 are Idaho, Oregon, and Utah. The averages are for homes valued at $125,000 or more. (Alaska, Hawaii, and Washington, DC, are not covered by the survey.)

Don't Be in Denial

Whether you're an owner or a renter, don't despair if you're having trouble getting an insurance company to issue you a residential policy. Most states make it illegal for an insurance company to refuse to sell you residential insurance based on your age, sex, race, creed, color, national origin, marital status, neighborhood, or occupation—unless of course that occupation is an illegal one like drug dealing. If you feel you are being denied coverage for any one of these reasons, immediately contact your state insurance department.

Now you are ready to get a handle on special situations such as insuring fine art, expensive jewelry, or that computer system complete with CD-ROM. Turn to chapter 10, where you will enter the realm of floaters and riders.

RENTERS and co-op owners are SPECIAL

The first step to getting a clue about renter's insurance is admitting that you need it. That said, let's look at why and how much!

You need renter's insurance if you rent a house or apartment and:

1. You have stereos, cameras, CD players, clothing, jewelry, sporting equipment, bicycles, televisions, or other valuables, and you can't afford to replace these items if they are stolen, damaged, or destroyed.

2. You can't afford to be sued.

Since almost nobody can afford to be sued, at the very least you need some renter's liability insurance.

Who Pays for Falling Trees?

During a ferocious hurricane, one of the trees on Joan Fletcher's property came crashing down on the house of her neighbor, Mark Tyson. Whose home insurance pays for the damage?

The answer may surprise you: Mark's. Generally, the rule is that the property owner whose house has been damaged by a tree is the one who files a claim with the insurance company. As long as the tree was in good health, and no one could have predicted its fall, then Joan is off the hook. Since in this case, the tree fell down on Mark's house because of a hurricane—an uncontrollable natural disaster—Joan can't be held responsible.

But what happens when a tree falls down because it was damaged or diseased? Then the situation becomes a lot more complicated. In this case, the property owner can try to hold the tree owner liable for the damages. If the property owner does sue the tree owner, then the tree owner's home insurance policy will pay for the defense and the damages, up to the policy limit.

So what should you do if you suspect that your neighbor's tree is damaged and is in danger of falling on your house? The best plan is to have a qualified person inspect the tree. If your expert determines that there is a problem, then he or she should write a letter to the tree owner, return receipt requested. This way, if the tree owner doesn't do anything to take care of the problem, and the tree does fall on your house, you're in the best shape to win a case against the tree owner.

If you're the one with the potentially problematic trees, then you should do everything possible to protect yourself against an expensive lawsuit from your neighbor. Have your trees maintained and examined each year, and consider taking them down if the expert finds a problem. If you don't want to take them down, then protect yourself with an umbrella policy that provides secondary coverage for legal liability, well above the limit of your homeowner's policy. This way, if worse comes to worst—the tree falls, and your neighbor sues—your insurance company will be covering the damages.

A renter's policy can protect your possessions, but you must make sure that you are insuring the possessions you want to insure and that you do not purchase too much insurance. Remember, if you rent, your landlord's insurance does not cover your personal property (clothes, stereo, furniture, and the like) against destruction or loss. You are responsible for insuring the contents of your apartment.

Consider what would happen if your upstairs neighbor left the bathroom faucet running and it flooded his apartment and yours—waterlogging your sofa, chairs, bed, and all your expensive electronic toys. Your landlord has no responsibility for putting right that damage. And don't rely on your neighbor's renter's insurance to cover you. Since only 41 percent of renters have insurance, chances are your neighbors don't have any. This is where your renter's insurance comes in. It's to make sure you are not left awash in bills to replace your damaged possessions.

The Perils of Renter's Insurance

The standard renter's policy—dubbed HO-4 in insurance industry lingo—protects you against losses due to a number of perils. Those perils are:

- Fire or smoke

- Lightning

- Vandalism

- Theft

- Explosion

- Windstorm

- Water damage from plumbing

Like standard homeowner's insurance, the perils of earthquakes and floods are not part of the standard renter's policy.

Renter's Insurance: The Fine Print

- *Replacement value*. Renter's insurance is also similar to homeowner's insurance in that you can upgrade it to cover the replacement value rather than the actual cash value of your belongings. The cost is only about 10 percent extra, but it probably is worth the extra dollars for that additional protection. Why is replacement insurance usually 10 percent extra for renters, but 15 percent extra for homeowners? This is because renters tend to have fewer belongings than homeowners. Moreover, it's harder to burglarize a renter because thieves usually have to get not only into the renter's apartment but also past the door of the apartment building.

- *Liability*. Renter's insurance does more than just cover your possessions. Like a homeowner's policy, it provides liability coverage as well. You'll be covered if someone is injured and then sues you. Make sure your policy also includes legal defense costs if you are taken to court.

- *Cost*. Basic renter's insurance is very affordable. It averages about $200 a year for a policy that gives you up to $40,000 worth of coverage on your belongings and another $300,000 of liability insurance with a $250 deductible.

Insurance with Your Roommates or "Significant Other"

If you live in a group house or share an apartment, you may still be able to buy renter's insurance. The regulations vary from state to state. Moreover, policies vary from company to company.

To get a handle on buying insurance with your roomies, start by calling your state insurance department and ask what regulations apply. Then start shopping: Check your yellow pages and Internet sites and concentrate on the top-rated firms in terms of their financial health and their service. Speak to some insurance agents—exclusive and independent.

Be aware that some insurance companies do not issue renter's policies for unmarried couples. Fortunately, others are more enlightened and do provide coverage. Some companies that will issue these policies are:

- Government Employees Insurance Co. (GEICO), One GEICO Blvd., Fredericksburg, VA 22412, (800) 841-3000

- St. Paul Fire & Marine Insurance, 385 Washington St., St. Paul, MN 55102, (800) 423-4545

- State Farm Insurance, One State Farm Plaza, Bloomington, IL 61701, (309) 766-2311

- USAA, 9800 Fredericksburg Rd., San Antonio, TX 78288, (800) 531-8100

Moreover, some policies automatically extend coverage to any future resident of a policyholder's household who fits the definition of domestic partner.

Condominium and Cooperative Owners

Homeowner's policies also exist for condo and co-op owners. The type of policy you'll need here, though, is determined by how much and what type of insurance the co-op or condo association already has. The insurance your association carries is part of your monthly condo or co-op fee and covers risk for common areas, outside structures, and liability outside your unit or apartment. You don't have a choice about paying it. Your share of this insurance bill is automatically part of your monthly fee.

The insurance you carry for your individual unit is your responsibility. Although you don't purchase this through the condo or co-op association, the managing agent may be able to recommend some insurance companies. Some association insurance covers units only to their bare walls—you're on your own when it comes to insurance for plumbing and wiring. Other associations cover these items as well. Check with yours to find out exactly what's covered before you purchase your own policy.

CONSIDER RENTER'S INSURANCE

Just like homeowner's insurance, renter's insurance covers your possessions against theft even if you take them out of your home. Many renters don't pay attention to this important benefit—and they end up regretting it. "I never really thought about renter's insurance," explained Matt Randall. "I didn't have a lot of expensive furniture, and I lived in a safe area, so I wasn't worried about break-ins."

Matt's job, however, does require him to travel on occasion. And during one business trip to San Francisco, he returned to his rental car to find that all his luggage had been stolen from the trunk. He immediately contacted his insurance company, but since he didn't have renter's insurance, there was nothing they could do. The result? Matt was forced to replace the luggage and its contents himself.

So think carefully about renter's insurance—it may come in handy when you least expect it.

At the very least, you need property insurance because the association's policy does not cover your possessions. You also need liability insurance because the association won't pay the damages or the legal expenses for the lawsuit you get slapped with if someone bangs his head on your open overhead kitchen cabinet, falls to the floor unconscious, dislocates his back, and ends up missing ten weeks of work. And finally, without insurance, if you knock over someone else's Waterford crystal and Limoges china, someone—and that someone is you—will have to replace it.

Read your association's insurance policy carefully. If you are unclear about what's covered, check with an association officer. Then fill in the gaps. Use the same method that a homeowner would to put a price tag on the value of everything inside the walls of your co-op or apartment. That includes not only your possessions but any upgrades you have made, like built-in cabinetry, custom-designed lighting, or built-out, space-saver closets.

In addition to getting recommendations from the managing agent, ask other unit owners for referrals to insurance companies or agents. The important thing is to understand the basics of residential insurance. After that, you merely have to find the right policy for your situation.

INSURANCE *for the* expensive *and* UNUSUAL

You need special policies to properly insure some of your expensive belongings such as jewelry, art, and your computer. Ditto for those rare but devastating events courtesy of Mother Nature— floods, earthquakes, and hurricanes— that may befall your home and possessions.

Quick now. List your three most valuable items: your sterling silver, an antique samovar, those signed nineteenth-century Japanese prints? A two-carat diamond ring, a Tiffany watch, a mink coat? Your Nikon camera, the buffalo nickel coin collection you inherited from Uncle Norman, your fax-packed, Internet/CD-ROM–loaded computer?

Well, guess what? Only a very small portion of the original value of these items is covered by your standard homeowner's insurance policy. Essentially, there are certain categories of valuable or unusual items that insurance companies won't insure with-

out collecting some extra premium from you. In order to be sure you are compensated for the loss of items like these, you need to buy extra insurance.

Just take a look at the maximum you could recoup from a standard homeowner's policy if these or other particularly pricey items are stolen or destroyed. It's not much.

- Money, gold, silver, and platinum (other than jewelry or flatware, coins, bank notes, and metals): $200

- Securities, deeds, manuscripts, tickets, stamps, and valuable financial papers such as letters of credit or evidence of debts owed to you: $1,000

- Watercraft, including trailers, furnishings, equipment, and outboard motors: $1,000

- Jewelry, watches, furs, and precious and semiprecious stones: $1,000 to $2,000

- Silverware, goldware, silver-plated or gold-plated ware, and pewterware: $2,500

- Firearms: $2,500

- Business equipment, such as computers, scanners, and duplicators used at home: $2,500 to $5,000

Some policies provide only limited coverage for:

- Artwork

- Antiques

- Musical instruments

- Cameras

- Golf equipment

- Oriental rugs

What's more, regular policies even further limit the amount you can collect within each category. For instance, let's say thieves swipe that $4,000 mink coat and your $2,500 Movado watch. You probably would not be able to collect $1,000 to $2,000 for the fur and another $1,000 to $2,000 for the timepiece. The most you could get would be $1,000 to $2,000 total, because the fur and the watch are in the same category, according to most insurance companies. Insurance companies limit coverage to these items in order to keep premiums at a reasonable level. Because most people don't own monstrously expensive watches and other high-ticket goodies, it's not cost-effective to build the cost of covering them into ordinary policies.

Fortunately, there is a way you can make sure these and other expensive items you own are covered a lot more fully. You can purchase additional protection called floaters or endorsements.

Enter the Realm of Floaters

The realm of residential insurance sports floaters, endorsements, and special policies to cover those really expensive possessions you cherish and value. These are totally separate policies from your residential insurance. They provide more insurance for your belongings and cover them against perils that are not part of your regular residential insurance.

Floaters are relatively inexpensive and are priced per $100 of coverage. The cost you will pay for a floater is determined by what you wish to insure and where you live. Big city dwellers pay more than small town or rural residents because the crime rate is higher in places like New York, Los Angeles, and Chicago than in Norwich, Connecticut, or Butte, Montana.

The neat thing about floaters, endorsements, and riders is that they cover just about every risk you can imagine, unless the policy specifically excludes something. Most floaters cover an item that is damaged or lost no matter how bizarre the situation. Thus, the coverage "floats" with the item.

This makes floater policies very different from regular residential policies which cover only named perils. With a floater, anything that is not specified is covered. With a standard residential policy, nothing is covered unless it is named.

With a floater policy, for instance, you are covered if your diamond tennis bracelet falls off your wrist and into the Atlantic Ocean while you are on the cruise ship to Bermuda or your Nikon camera gets ripped off your shoulder while walking on the Ipanema beach in Rio de Janeiro. And, if your best friend's toddler applies paint to your mink coat during the eggnog party you throw every December, a floater will pay to have your coat repaired.

What's Being Floated?

The trick to buying floater policies is to determine the value of the items you want to insure. For jewelry and artwork, for example, that means you'll need to get a professional appraisal. A written appraisal puts a dollar value on the item at the time of the appraisal and includes a detailed description of the item.

Where do you find an appraiser? Your best and most inexpensive solution is to get a written appraisal at the time of the sale from the place you bought the item. Sometimes, the jeweler or art dealer will supply you with an appraisal free of charge.

If you didn't get an appraisal at the time of purchase, you can take your ring or bracelet to a good jeweler to get the necessary documents. Art dealers and auction houses can also provide appraisals. Ask your insurance agent for the names of a couple of appraisers you might use. The appraiser will either charge you a flat or hourly fee, which could range anywhere from $75 to $500 an hour, depending on the item and where you live.

Get written documentation for the items you want to insure. For sterling silver flatware, the value may vary, depending on the commodity price of silver at the time, but the items in your Tiffany silver pattern have a specific, set price. Here, it's important to record the specific number of teaspoons, salad forks, and butter knives you have.

There's no getting around the fact that this is a tedious task—but it's not difficult. You may be very surprised at just how much you own—and therefore, how much you stand to lose if you don't insure with a floater. In addition to a written record of these items, it's a good idea to take photos. Do keep your records in a safe location. The best and most secure place is a safe deposit box at a bank.

No Coverage for the Sentiment

You may be surprised to discover that the intricately filigreed gold brooch you treasure from your grandmother's inheritance is worth only $550. While you may place great sentimental value on it, you won't be able to insure it for any more than that. Moreover, some insurance companies won't even issue you a floater policy unless an item has a minimum value. For instance, art objects must have a minimum value of $250.

Fur coats, unlike silver or jewelry, do not maintain their value. The $4,000 mink you bought six years ago is probably worth a lot less today. Consult a furrier as to its current value. Unfortunately, that's the maximum for which you can insure it under a standard residential policy. A floater, though, would replace the coat with a similar used or "previously owned" fur. If the coat is damaged, a floater policy will pay for the repair cost up to the current value of the coat.

Press "Enter" for Computer Insurance

Yes. You can get insurance for your computer. It's not hard to do and it's not expensive. Better still, computer insurance covers a variety of mishaps and missteps.

Special insurance for your computer covers such standard disasters as fire, volcanic eruptions, and windstorm damage. It also covers damage to the computer if you spill that bottle of Snapple onto the keyboard, shorting out the circuitry and causing the system to go dead. You're covered as well if you stick your laptop on the seat in the airport boarding area, only to discover ten minutes later that while you were engrossed in reading *The Wall Street Journal* your computer has been snatched. You can even be covered if you just plain leave it in the taxi and no one turns it into the Yellow Cab lost-and-found.

Why not rely on your basic residential policy for computer insurance? The reason is that the policy probably covers no more than $250 for the laptop you take out of your house and may cover nothing for that klutzy move with the Snapple. And for the entire system that the burglar steals from your home, you may be covered for a maximum of $2,500 minus the deductible on your homeowner's or renter's policy. If the system is a couple of years old, you might be reimbursed for even less than that.

HERE AN APPRAISER, THERE AN APPRAISER

Clueless about where to go to get that samovar appraised? Not to worry. Rather than sorting through the listings in the yellow pages, you can contact:

American Society of Appraisers
Box 17265
Washington, DC 20041
(800) 272-8258

Appraisers Association of America
386 Park Ave. South
Suite 2000
New York, NY 10016
(212) 889-5404

These organizations can help you locate an appraiser in your area for the specific item or items that need to be valued and documented.

Only a few insurance companies have pioneered in the emerging field of computer insurance. Many others are in the process of developing floater policies for computers.

Safeware of Columbus, Ohio, specializes in just this kind of protection. Safeware's Computer-owner's Insurance Policy costs as little as $49 a year for $2,000 worth of coverage with a $50 deductible or as much as $159 a year for $17,000 worth of coverage. Laptop insurance costs $96 for $3,000 in coverage with a $50 deductible. (If you live in New York, Florida, Mississippi, Texas, and area codes 215 and 610 in Pennsylvania, the coverage varies and premiums are higher.) Give them a call at (614) 262-0559. The policy offers full replacement for hardware and purchased software. It covers fire, theft (but not from an unattended vehicle—so you can't leave it in the car), power surges, accidental damages (the Snapple snafu, for instance), vandalism, and natural disasters such as lightning and floods (but not earthquakes).

RLI Insurance in Peoria, Illinois, (309) 692-1000, offers a comprehensive, in-home business policy in all 50 states. The policy covers theft, damage, fire, and power surges. It also covers laptops. Premiums range in price from $150 to $280 a year, the equipment limit is $5,000. The policy includes data recovery costs and pays out up to $1,000 for the cost to research, replace, and restore lost information.

A benefit not often sought but nice to have is coverage for the loss of business income. This means that if your clients go elsewhere while you are busy restoring your lost data, RLI will cover you for that lost income. The benefit amount fluctuates based on your income and expenses and has a year-long limit.

RLI offers a rider to the policy that pays for replacement rather than actual cash value. This is one area of your computer insurance policy's fine print that you need to inspect closely. Like your home and possessions covered in your regular homeowner's policy, you want replacement—not cash value—in your computer insurance policy. With computers constantly being made cheaper and more powerful, you want to be sure your insurance coverage will let you replace what you had without having to settle for an inferior product. Typically, it costs about 10 to 15 percent more to upgrade from actual cash value to replacement coverage. It's worth the price.

Lions and Tigers and Bears—or Earthquakes, Tornadoes, and Floods

Standard homeowner's insurance policies do not cover flooding. Fortunately, you may be able to buy flood insurance, depending on where you live, outside your basic home-owner's policy. It's available through the National Flood Insurance Program (NFIP) administered by Uncle Sam's Federal Emergency Management Agency (FEMA).

To get flood insurance, though, your community has to participate in the NFIP. That means it must abide by some very specific rules for the flood-prone areas in the community. Call (800) 638-6620 to find out if your community is part of NFIP. If your community does not participate in the federal program, you cannot obtain flood insurance. The one exception is that some mobile homeowner's policies do insure against the peril of a flood. If you don't live in a mobile home and your area is not a NFIP participant, forget about flood insurance.

If your home is located in a participating community, you can apply for flood insurance through any licensed property/casualty insurance agent, including your home-owner's agent. Another source is the "Write Your Own" program through which major insurance companies sell flood insurance that is approved by FEMA and subsidized by the U.S. government, but issued under the company name. Once you apply, there may be a five-day waiting period before the coverage becomes effective.

WHY PRIVATE HOMEOWNER'S INSURANCE DOES NOT COVER FLOODS

Private homeowner's insurance does not cover flood damage because most people don't need it. Thus, it wouldn't be fair to charge them for it. That's what insurance company executives say.

Of course, the people who do need it and would buy it are likely to have a loss. Thus, the insurance companies can't figure out a way to make money on flood insurance. That's why the federal government steps in with its own policies. The financial risk is shared by all the citizens of the United States.

The cost of flood insurance varies depending on the location of your property and how susceptible it is to flooding. You can buy a policy for coverage of up to $185,000 for your home and $60,000 for your belongings.

Your dwelling and your belongings are covered by separate policies and there are minimum deductibles for each. The minimums will be either $500 or $750 depending on where your property is located. As with other types of insurance, you can lower the cost—the premium—by raising the deductible level.

You can insure your home against flooding for the replacement cost as long as your dwelling is your primary residence for 80 percent of the calendar year. Thus, cash value is the only flood insurance option for a vacation home.

Condominium and cooperative associations can also buy flood insurance through the NFIP. As an individual unit owner, you, too, can purchase a separate policy to protect your belongings against flood damage. Remember, the association's policy insures your unit's walls, floors, and ceilings, but won't cover your furniture, clothing, and other possessions.

What's Not Covered

Even if you get flood insurance, there are still some things that are not covered:

- Fences, pools, boathouses, docks, land, shrubs, septic tanks, walks, patios, driveways, animals, motorized vehicles, recreational vehicles, and business property

- Rain damage, sewer backup, or water seepage that occurs at some time other than when the flood happened

- Loss of access, loss of use, loss of profits from your at-home business, or an increased cost to repair or reconstruct due to any laws or ordinances that regulate these items

- The finished parts of your basement such as paneling and linoleum as well as contents such as rugs and furniture

There is also a $250 total limit on items such as paintings, art, jewelry, furs, and precious metal that are damaged as a result of a flood.

Earthquakes

Unlike flood insurance, earthquake insurance is available for you to purchase as you wish, in the form of an addendum to your standard homeowner's policy. That's just about the only news that's good when it comes to earthquake insurance.

Earthquake insurance can be expensive and it carries huge deductibles. The cost depends on where you live and the type of home you live in. For example, you may pay $6,000 a year for a $500,000 policy on a brick home in California, but only $630 for a frame home in the same area because frame homes withstand earthquake tremors better than brick ones. As a renter in New York City, though, you may be able to get a policy that costs $4 for every $10,000 of coverage for the belongings in your apartment.

For you, the big shock—after the tremor—may be just how little earthquake insurance pays because the deductible is sky high. Earthquake insurance usually carries a deductible of 10 percent of the value of the policy. Thus, the bigger the policy, the more you have to pay before the insurance company starts forking over the money.

Let's say you insure your house for $200,000 and your belongings for $100,000. Your 10 percent deductible would then be $20,000 for the house and $10,000 for your belongings. That's $30,000 out of your pocket before you start collecting.

Your best bet, even with the big deductible, is to buy a guaranteed replacement policy. Make sure it is guaranteed, not just a policy for replacement value. The reason is

that when an earthquake occurs, the cost to rebuild and replace skyrockets since local construction firms know they can charge premium rates. A guaranteed replacement policy covers the cost—minus the deductible—even if the replacement cost exceeds the stated value of the policy.

If you live in an area that's prone to severe earthquakes, this insurance makes sense for you. Otherwise this may be one of those extras you want to skip.

Windstorms, Hurricanes, and Tornadoes

Windstorms—and that includes hurricanes and tornadoes—are covered by your standard homeowner's policy. Still, you may need additional coverage.

Hurricanes fell trees and power lines, blow out windows, and lift off roofs. A lot of damage can be done by the flooding that accompanies hurricanes. Thus, you may be eligible to get flood insurance—if your area is covered by the National Flood Insurance Program.

Moreover, seven states—Alabama, Florida, Louisiana, Mississippi, North Carolina, South Carolina, and Texas—also provide special insurance plans to cover hurricane damage. Call one of the following special underwriting associations to find out how you can get insurance to cover hurricane damage if you live in one of these seven states. Once you have all of the information about coverage and cost in hand, you can purchase a policy directly from the underwriting association, or you can contact your insurance company.

- Alabama Insurance Underwriting Association, 315 East Laurel Ave., Suite 216 D, Foley, AL 36535, (334) 943-4029

- Florida Windstorm Underwriting Association, One Liberty Center, 7077 Bonneval Rd., Jacksonville, FL 32216, (904) 296-6105

- Louisiana Insurance Underwriting Association, P.O. Box 60730, New Orleans, LA 70160, (504) 527-0833

If You Live in California...

There is a greater chance for an earthquake to ruin your home in California than any other state in the country. State law mandates that insurance companies that sell residential policies also sell earthquake insurance. But in the aftermath of the Big Quake of 1994, many insurance companies—anticipating that another major quake would wipe them out—stopped selling earthquake policies. Because there is no federally funded earthquake insurance program like the National Flood Insurance Program, it became difficult for California residents to obtain earthquake coverage.

Although individual insurance companies have started to offer earthquake insurance again, 70 percent of the policies written today are through the California Earthquake Authority (CEA), which was established by the state to enable insurance companies to spread this hefty risk. CEA is a state-regulated, 13-member organization of private insurance companies funded partly by premiums, partly by the member companies, and partly by reinsurance, a form of insurance for insurance companies. Premiums and coverage are comparable to policies sold by individual insurance companies. To obtain CEA insurance, use the yellow pages to contact one of the member companies listed below:

- Allstate Indemnity
- Armed Forces Insurance Exchange
- Automobile Club of Southern California
- California FAIR Plan
- CNA
- Continental Insurance
- CSAA
- Farmers Group

- Liberty Mutual
- Mercury
- Midwest Mutual
- Preferred Risk
- Prudential
- State Farm Fire and Casualty
- State Farm General
- USAA
- USAA Casualty

Do You Need Business Insurance?

If you are a small business owner (home-based or otherwise), there are some special insurance considerations you need to make. Business insurance could be the subject of its own book, but here are some tips about how to figure out if you need it. Check with your insurance agent. Let her know about your business situation and she can suggest the types of added insurance you'll need to consider. If she doesn't specialize in business insurance, find yourself an agent who does before you actually buy any coverage. Here are some of the things your agent might mention to you.

• *Insurance for bank loans.* If you plan to secure some kind of financing for your business, be prepared to cough up some dough to insure the lender against the loss of the collateral you use to secure the loan.

• *State and federal law.* These laws require you provide unemployment and worker's compensation coverage for employees if you have any. Contact your state worker's compensation board to find out how to secure it and how much you need to buy.

• *Health benefits.* Although it's not required by law, many companies provide employees with some kind of health coverage. And, if you have more than 100 employees and provide any of them with any kind of group insurance, federal law requires you to offer it to all workers.

• *Business auto insurance.* If your employees drive as part of their job, then you need to have this kind of coverage in case they have an accident while working for you. This will cover them (and you) even if they're just using their cars to run errands or drive themselves to the airport to take a business trip for you.

• *Liability.* Almost every industry is exposed to special types of liability. For example, if you run a small public relations firm, you'll need to purchase special liability insurance to cover you if you get sued for slanderous comments you make in a press release. Make sure you know what types of insurance are standard coverage for other businesses in your industry.

• *Employee liability.* If you have employees working for you, make sure you carry extra liability to cover you for anything that may happen to them or damage that they might do to someone else's property while they're on the job.

• *Product liability.* If you manufacture a product, insure yourself against any lawsuits that may arise due to someone being injured while using your product. Your product may not be to blame, but you'll still incur some hefty legal bills proving that in a court of law.

• *Business interruption insurance.* You can buy insurance that will reimburse you for any loss of business income you may incur due to some event interfering with the operation of your business (such as a fire or theft).

Where to learn more about business insurance:

• *How to Start and Run a Successful Consulting Business* by Gregory and Patricia Kishel, published by John Wiley & Sons, 1996.

• *Insurance Smart: How to Buy the Right Insurance at the Right Price* by Jeff O'Donnell, published by John Wiley & Sons, 1991. A no-holds-barred primer on selecting all kinds of insurance by a veteran agent.

- Mississippi Windstorm Underwriting Association, P.O. Box 5389, 2685 Insurance Center Dr., Jackson, MI 39296, (601) 981-2915

- North Carolina Joint Underwriting Association, 1700 Hillsborough St., Raleigh, NC 27605, (919) 821-1299

- South Carolina Windstorm and Hail Underwriting Association, P.O. Box 407, Columbia, SC 29202, (803) 779-8373

- Texas Catastrophe Property Insurance Association, P.O. Box 2930, Austin, TX 78768, (512) 444-9612

The Big Key

Do remember that the key to getting the best value for the dollars you spend for a floater for your jewelry, special coverage for your computer, or a policy to cover floods is to look for guaranteed replacement value. If you can't get that, opt for replacement value coverage. This type of insurance gives you the protection you need should a big—or even little—disaster come your way.

STEERING
your way
to the right
AUTO POLICY

CHAPTER ELEVEN

Some people spend more time in their cars than they do in their homes. Maybe that's why most states require some sort of car insurance. This chapter will steer you gear-by-gear through your options so you can get this part of your insurance structure in place.

You need auto insurance because you are financially responsible for your actions behind the wheel of a vehicle. If you injure someone, your insurance pays for their medical bills. If you damage your car or someone else's, your insurance pays the repair bills. If you become injured, your insurance pays for your own medical bills. And if someone sues you as a result of an accident, your insurance pays the legal fees and any damages you may end up owing, up to a limit. Without insurance, you have to pay all these costs yourself. Moreover, all states require car insurance—but there's a gap between what many of them require and what you really need.

There are actually six parts to your auto insurance policy:

1. Bodily injury liability

2. Property damage liability

3. Collision

4. Comprehensive

5. Medical payments

6. Uninsured motorist's coverage

Each covers something different, and in fact, you can buy them separately. Your best bet always—repeat, always—is to buy them from the same insurance company. If you don't, you're likely to pay a lot more for your insurance than you have to. In fact, when you talk to insurance agents about your car, they're likely to lump all six parts together in your conversation. But it's important for you to know what they are and what they cover.

Keep in mind that auto insurance falls into two broad categories—property coverage for damage to your car and liability coverage for damage to someone else and their property. Some states require that you carry certain types of coverage, such as an uninsured motorist policy. The level of liability insurance you have to carry is also mandated by the state in which you have registered your car. But don't let the government tell you how much auto insurance you should have. More often than not, the state minimums are too low to protect you sufficiently.

Your own situation should determine the level of coverage you buy. The more assets you have to protect, the more liability protection you will need. The size and make-up of your family is another factor. For instance, if you are a single 39-year-old woman who drives rarely and has never even been in a fender bender, you probably need a lot less liability coverage than a 39-year-old married woman with two teenaged boys who recently passed their driving tests and are now covered on Mom and Dad's auto policy. Remember, it takes just one accident accompanied by one whopping lawsuit to wipe out a lifetime of assets if you are not properly covered in the liability arena.

Notifying Your Insurer about a New Car

If you own two cars—even if you're the only person who drives either of them—you still have to report both of them to your auto insurer. Frank Carter found that out the hard way.

Frank lived year-round in Massachusetts until 1989, when he retired and started spending his winters in Florida. During his first trip down to Florida, he decided that it was time to purchase a second car to keep in Florida.

The problem? Frank never notified his insurer that he had bought a second car. He renewed his umbrella liability insurance policy on his first car (a 1981 Chevy) without ever telling them about his new car (a 1971 Ford). "I didn't see why it made a difference," explained Frank. "After all, when I'm in Massachusetts, I only use the Chevy. And when I'm in Florida, I only use the Ford. No one else drives either car. So there's only one car in use at any given time."

Unfortunately, his insurance company didn't see it quite like that. And when Frank got into an accident with his Ford in Florida, the insurance company refused to pay, claiming that Frank had misrepresented his car ownership. Since insurers almost always charge a higher premium for two cars—even if only one car can be used at a time—Frank's premiums would have gone up slightly if he had been honest on his insurance forms. And since he didn't pay the higher premium, the insurance company didn't have to pay for him.

Remember the Clueless guideline: Insurers will almost always look for a way to get out of paying your claim. Don't provide them with an easy opportunity to do that.

Sifting through the mishmash of the six parts, what's required, and what you want as coverage can be a tedious task, for sure. But it is not brain twisting. Getting the best deal on the auto insurance you need and want consists of five easy steps. They are:

1. Get familiar with what the six options cover.

2. Determine what your state requires.

3. Determine what you want in coverage—over and above what your state mandates.

4. Decide what kind of deductibles you want. As with other types of insurance, the higher your deductibles, the lower your premiums.

5. Determine the discounts to which you are entitled for items such as a good driving record.

6. Comparison shop for quotes.

Now let's take a look at the six specific parts of your auto policy.

Bodily Injury Liability

Bodily injury liability provides coverage in case you cause an accident in which someone else is injured or killed. It also pays for your legal defense if someone sues you. This type of insurance is required in all states. There is no deductible.

Unfortunately, though, the state limits are usually too low to protect you well. For example, California requires that you only carry a 15/30 policy. That's insurance jargon meaning up to $15,000 worth of coverage for each injured person involved and up to a total payout of $30,000 per accident. If you're only carrying the minimum and you are sued to the tune of $250,000 for an accident you caused, your insurance company will only pay out $30,000. You'll be personally responsible for the rest.

The recommended coverage for bodily injury liability is at least $100,000 worth of liability coverage for each person who may be hurt in an accident that you cause and up to a $300,000 total per accident. This is known as 100/300 and is the most typical

coverage offered by the auto insurance industry. Purchasing even more bodily liability insurance won't increase your premium by all that much, so if you can swing it, consider purchasing a 250/500 policy.

Property Damage Liability

This is for damage to someone else's property. Usually the damage involved is done to another car, but this insurance also covers other types of property such as buildings or lampposts. It also pays for legal defense costs. It covers you, members of your family, and anyone you give permission to drive your car. There is no deductible.

For example, let's say you have a Super Bowl party. At halftime, you ask a friend to drive your car to the local convenience store for more chips and dip. On the way, your friend mistakenly shifts into reverse rather than first gear, slams your car into someone else's auto, does a 90-degree spin, and smashes into your neighbor's family room. Within limits, your insurance covers any injury your friend incurs (that's covered by the bodily liability just mentioned) and any damage to the other car involved, as well as your neighbor's family room, up to the limit specified in your policy.

Buy at least $50,000 of property damage coverage on each car you are insuring. The state minimum requirements can be as low as $5,000. Often that $5,000 will not cover the cost to repair or replace a car or the wrecked family room.

When insurance industry people talk about liability coverage—bodily injury and property damage—they roll the coverage into three figures. They talk about 100/300/50 coverage, for instance, dropping zeros along the way. The first two numbers refer to bodily liability as discussed earlier, while the third number covers the property damage liability. Here's what the numbers mean:

- The first number is for bodily injury liability per person. It's $100,000 in our example.

- The second is for bodily injury liability per accident. It's $300,000 total for any one accident in this example.

- The third is for property damage. It's $50,000 for any one accident in this example.

Different states have different minimum requirements for liability insurance. Consult the table on page 153 for the state in which you live, but also check your local insurance company because these requirements are subject to change. If you live in New Jersey, for example, the liability limits are 15/30/5. This means New Jersey requires that you have a minimum of $15,000 bodily injury coverage per person, $30,000 bodily injury coverage per accident, and $5,000 property damage coverage. Remember, this just covers your liability to someone else. It does not cover any damage you do to yourself or your car.

Collision Insurance

Collision pays for the damage to your car as a result of any kind of collision, be it with another car, a cement wall, or a lamppost, whether or not it was your fault. Even if a thief steals your car and totals it, your insurance company will pay for the repairs at the body shop.

Collision insurance carries a deductible, and the maximum you can collect for repair costs is limited to the value of your car prior to the collision minus the deductible. In other words, suppose you total your car, which is valued at $2,500 according to the auto industry's *Kelley Blue Book*, and you're carrying a $500 deductible. If the cost of the repair is more than $2,000, the insurance company won't pay for it. They'll "total out" your car, and cut you a check for $2,000 (the value of your car minus your deductible).

Collision insurance is optional—it isn't mandated by state law. So you need to consider carefully whether or not you need it. Weigh the value of your car against the premium you have to pay to cover it.

Add the deductible to the cost of the collision insurance for the car. If that number exceeds the market value of your car, collision insurance is a waste of your money because you will be paying out more than you can ever collect if you have an accident that totals your car. If the deductible and collision insurance combined are less than the value of your car, collision insurance makes sense.

Remember, the cost of collision insurance is determined by the value of your car, or how much it would cost to replace it if it were totaled in an accident. Collision coverage for your one-year-old Volvo is going to cost a lot more than collision for your ten-year-old Chevy Nova. As your car ages, however, the cost to replace it goes down, so before renewing your policy every year, reassess whether or not it makes sense to keep the collision coverage.

Comprehensive Insurance

Comprehensive reimburses you if your car is stolen and for damages to your car caused by something other than a collision. The perils covered by comprehensive insurance are fire, theft, missiles and falling objects, explosions, earthquakes, floods, riots, and civil commotions. It also covers damages to your car if you hit an animal such as a deer or if your car is overturned during a natural disaster or riot.

Comprehensive coverage is not required by state law. How much you carry is up to you, but like collision, you should never insure your car for more than its actual cash or market value.

Use the same formula for comprehensive insurance that you used for collision insurance to determine when you need it and, more important, when you can drop this coverage. Just because your insurance company is still billing you for comprehensive insurance doesn't mean that you automatically need it.

Here's what you do. Call your agent and ask what the current market value of your car actually is, and how much of your total auto premium is going toward the comprehensive portion. Hang up the phone and make your calculations. If it doesn't make economic sense to carry comprehensive, call the agent back, say you want to drop the comprehensive coverage, and ask that a new bill be sent to you reflecting this change. If you have miscalculated and still need comprehensive coverage, your agent probably will quickly note any error you have made. If your numbers are correct, the agent will gladly alter your coverage.

Medical Payments Insurance

This pays the medical bills, disability, and lost wages—and even the funeral costs—as a result of an auto accident, no matter who is at fault. It covers you, members of your family, and passengers in your car. It offers even broader medical and other coverage

PAY PREMIUMS ON TIME

There are some bills in life you can pay late—and some you can't. Insurance premiums fall into the second camp. If you're late with a premium, you set in motion a chain of events that could put your coverage in jeopardy. Most insurance companies allow a grace period and will not cancel a policy immediately if your payment is late. In fact, such immediate cancellation is outlawed in most states.

But if you are late, the company will probably send you a notice of nonpayment, giving you a date by which the payment must be made. If you don't make that payment—even if the check is in the mail—your policy will lapse and you will suddenly be exposed to the very perils you're trying to insure against.

There's another risk to being late with payments: If it happens consistently, your insurer may decide not to renew your policy.

to you and members of your family than your regular health insurance. This type of Personal Injury Protection (PIP) is required in states that have no-fault laws, and can also be purchased even if you do not live in a no-fault state.

Whose Fault Is No-Fault?

The core of no-fault insurance law is really easy to understand. Just remember that state law mandates whether its insurance system operates under a fault or no-fault system. So always ask your agent what kind of state you live in before purchasing auto insurance.

Under a no-fault system, state law dictates that your insurance company must pay your accident insurance claim whether or not the accident was your fault. In "fault" states, the insurance company of the person who was at fault pays the insurance claims. Of course, you may have to file a lawsuit to prove that you were not at fault for the accident.

Obviously, you're better protected under a no-fault system. If someone else causes an accident and you're in a fault state, you'd better hope they have insurance. If they don't, you're out of luck unless you can sue them for damages. That's where uninsured motorist's insurance comes into play.

Uninsured Motorist's

This coverage pays for injuries to you and passengers in your car if you are hit by someone who does not have insurance. You also are covered if you get clobbered by a hit-and-run driver.

State Auto Insurance Liability Limits

(Bodily injury per person/Bodily injury per accident/Property damage)

State	Limits	State	Limits
Alabama	20/40/10	Nebraska	25/50/25
Alaska	50/100/25	Nevada	10/15/30
Arizona	15/30/10	New Hampshire	25/50/25
Arkansas	25/50/15	New Jersey	15/30/5
California	15/30/5	New Mexico	25/50/25
Colorado	25/50/15	New York	*25/50/10
Connecticut	20/40/10	North Carolina	25/50/15
Delaware	15/30/10	North Dakota	25/50/25
District of Columbia	25/50/10	Ohio	12.5/25/7.5
Florida	10/0/10	Oklahoma	10/20/10
Georgia	15/30/10	Oregon	25/50/10
Hawaii	25/0/10	Pennsylvania	15/30/5
Idaho	25/50/15	Rhode Island	25/50/25
Illinois	20/40/15	South Carolina	15/30/5
Indiana	25/50/10	South Dakota	25/50/25
Iowa	20/40/15	Tennessee	20/50/10
Kansas	25/50/10	Texas	20/40/15
Kentucky	25/50/10	Utah	25/50/15
Louisiana	10/20/10	Vermont	20/40/10
Maine	20/40/10	Virginia	25/50/20
Maryland	20/40/10	Washington	25/50/10
Massachusetts	20/40/5	West Virginia	20/40/10
Michigan	20/40/10	Wisconsin	25/50/25
Minnesota	30/60/10	Wyoming	25/50/20
Mississippi	10/20/5		
Missouri	25/50/10	*50/100 if injury results in death	
Montana	25/50/5		

Collision and Comprehensive Insurance Worksheet

Don't carry collision or comprehensive for more than the market value of your car minus the deductible and the cost of the insurance premium.

Insurance	Required	Your Choice
Amount of Collision	No, Optional	_____
$ 100 Deductible (Y/N)	_____	_____
$ 250 Deductible (Y/N)	_____	_____
$ 500 Deductible (Y/N)	_____	_____
$1,000 Deductible (Y/N)	_____	_____
Amount of Comprehensive	No, Optional	_____
Zero Deductible (Y/N)	_____	_____
$ 50 Deductible (Y/N)	_____	_____
$100 Deductible (Y/N)	_____	_____

This type of insurance is mandatory in some states. Whether required or not, uninsured motorist's insurance is essential if you live in a densely populated area where lots of people drive uninsured. It's a good idea to buy a policy that covers $100,000 for each person and $300,000 per accident.

Even if you live in a no-fault state, you still need to consider uninsured motorist's coverage. If you collide with an uninsured motorist, the insurance company is only responsible for paying out the state-mandated liability minimums, which as you've already seen, can be very low. Uninsured motorist's coverage increases the payout to make sure you get the care you need.

Tally the Discounts

There are loads of discounts available on auto insurance and each and every one can lower your premiums. Not all companies, though, offer all of these discounts. Be ever watchful—the amount of the discount will vary from policy to policy within the same insurance company. If any of these apply to you, call your insurance company to see if it offers discounts:

- If you put more than one car on a policy you may be eligible for a 15 to 20 percent discount.

- If any of the drivers in your household have been accident-free or have had no moving violations for the past three years, you may qualify for a discount.

- Discounts of 10 to 20 percent are available for drivers 50 years old or older who drive a limited number of miles per year.

- Young people who take high school driver training courses and people 50 years old and older who have completed driver training

PIP COVERS DRIVE-BY SHOOTINGS

In 1991, Tuan Van Le was a victim of a drive-by shooting while he was a passenger in a car. He was paralyzed from the waist down as a result of his injuries and filed claims. Although he was unable to collect under the uninsured motorist's protection policy, he was granted over $50,000 from Farmers Texas County Mutual Insurance, Allstate Indemnity, and State Farm, under the PIP portion of their policies, according to a Texas court ruling.

courses offered by the American Association of Retired Persons may qualify for discounts.

- You may qualify for a 5 to 15 percent discount if you make it harder for thieves to steal your car by installing an ignition cutoff system, an alarm system, a tracking system, or a hood- and wheel-locking device.

- Drivers of any age who don't rack up big miles are eligible for discounts. If you drive your car fewer than 7,000 miles per year, let your agent know.

- If your car is equipped with automatic seat belts and air bags, you may be able to reduce the premium for your medical payments insurance.

- Antilock brakes improve steering control and stability when you bring your car to a stop, thus reducing accidents. Some states—including Florida and New York—require insurers to give discounts for cars with antilock brakes. Even without such a mandate, some insurance companies offer discounts for these devices.

- A student with a B average or better may be eligible for a discount.

- If your college kid lives away from home and doesn't have a car, you may be eligible for a discount on your car insurance.

- If your homeowner's or renter's insurance and auto insurance are with the same company, you may get a discount on all the policies.

Time to Go Shopping

Now you are ready to start shopping for insurance. This too involves a couple of steps. Take one at a time to get the job done.

Step One: Eliminate the Negative

As with shopping for residential insurance, you start your auto insurance shopping by eliminating certain companies. Shop for auto insurance only from a firm with at least an "A" rating from the insurance rating services.

Your next eliminating step involves scratching off those companies with a bad service and/or payment record. For the service record, consult the issue of *Consumer Reports* that rates the companies' service from best to worst. Call (914) 378-2000 to find out in which issue the ratings appear.

One last task involves getting information from your state's insurance department. Ask for a "complaint ratio" listing of the auto insurance companies operating in your state. The lower the ratio, the fewer complaints that have been lodged against the company in relation to the total amount of policies the company has issued in your state. A high complaint ratio indicates consumers have had problems with the company. Avoid these firms so that you don't become just another statistic in next year's report.

Step Two: Get Quotes

Get out those auto insurance worksheets on pages 154, 158, and 159. Make sure the list of possible discounts is handy too. Now, you can get down to the business of getting prices for the insurance you want. Here are some suggestions for your comparison shopping.

Start with the biggest and most well-established insurance companies, such as State Farm and Allstate. Then, consult the yellow pages for insurance companies and agents in your area. Ask them for quotes. Also, start collecting as much background information as possible. Ask for any brochures and financial statements, such as an annual report, about the insurance company underwriting the policy you are considering. Don't let an agent pressure you into buying insurance on the spot. Review the literature and get quotes from at least three different firms.

Then branch out beyond the local scene. Use the Internet. Access the auto insurance company home pages. You'll find these Web site addresses in the resources section on page 210. Call some direct marketers who only sell over the phone and through the mail. Two of these are USAA at (800) 531-8100 and GEICO at (800) 841-3000.

Be sure to ask all these companies to provide quotes for the same coverage and don't forget to ask about those discounts.

Your Medical Payments Insurance, Personal Injury Protection (PIP), and Uninsured Motorist's Insurance Worksheet

If you have good health, life, and disability insurance coverage, you probably only need the minimum required coverage for PIP in a no-fault state, and no coverage at all in a state that doesn't require no-fault insurance.

Insurance	Required Min./ Mandatory	Your Choice
Medical Payments	No, Optional	_____
Personal Injury Protection	_____	_____
You live in a no-fault state	_____	_____
Don't live in a no-fault state	No, Optional	_____
Uninsured Motorist's Coverage	_____	_____

Personal Injury Protection coverage is required in the following states:

- Colorado
- Connecticut
- Delaware
- Florida
- Georgia
- Hawaii
- Kansas
- Kentucky*
- Maryland
- Massachusetts
- Michigan
- Minnesota
- New Jersey*
- New York
- North Dakota
- Oregon
- Pennsylvania*
- Puerto Rico
- Utah

*In the starred states, you have a choice as to whether you want to be part of the fault or no-fault system. If you opt out of the no-fault system, you may have to file a lawsuit to determine who was at fault in an auto accident. The positive aspect of a fault system is that if you are not at fault for an accident, you may be able to sue the other driver's insurance company for more damages than you would have received under the no-fault system.

Your Bodily Injury and Property Damage Liability Insurance Worksheet

Insurance	Required Min.	Your Choice
Bodily Injury Liability		
Per person	_____	_____
Per accident	_____	_____
Property Damage Liability	_____	_____

Step Three: Tally the Numbers

Once you have filled out these columns for each company, tally the results with your handy pocket calculator. Then, before you sign the contract, recheck to make sure your prospective insurance company's financial health and service record are top-notch.

Things Change

As with any insurance, you may have to adjust the amount and kind of car insurance you carry to be sure it responds to any changes in your situation. If your daughter turns 16 and starts driving, you must notify the insurance company. If you don't and she has an accident in your car, that particular accident would be covered, but the insurance company might drop your coverage after that or at the least refuse to renew you when your policy expires.

If you take a little bit of time to review your policy once a year, you'll probably end up saving money. For example, unless you purchase a new car every year, the value of your old one will decrease and you can reduce the amount of comprehensive insurance you carry on it. Do your audit in September or October, soon after the new model-year cars are introduced. No matter when you bought your car, its practical birthday—for insurance purposes—is when the new models appear in the dealer showrooms.

Review the list of discounts. Your kids may have raised their grade-point averages to qualify for good student discounts. You may have reached age 50. If you move to a house with a secure garage rather than only a driveway, you might be able to reduce your premium.

All this attention to details can garner you dollar savings—the little bit of time you invest will definitely be worth the money.

YOU bet your life INSURANCE

CHAPTER TWELVE

Not everyone needs life insurance. But if you do, make sure whatever policy you buy will be able to take care of your family and the financial obligations you'd leave behind should you die. Think of this as the ceiling of your total insurance program.

Life insurance is different from the other types of insurance for three reasons:

1. Buying life insurance is a selfless act because it isn't designed to take care of you. Your beneficiaries—the people who benefit by collecting—are the people you leave behind when you die. You buy life insurance to take care of your family and the obligations that may prove to be a financial burden to them. Unfortunately, many people lose track of this basic principle and they either end up spending too much on life insurance they don't need or they buy the wrong type.

2. With health, disability, residential, and auto insurance, a risk exists but it's not a certainty. You may have an auto accident in which you seriously injure someone else, but you may also go through your driving life with nothing more than a minor $500 fender bender. You may have a rare disease that cuts your earnings to zero, but then again you may be relatively healthy save for an isolated kidney stone attack, a sprained ankle, and periodic bouts of the flu. Insurance covers the risk—not the certainty—of those events occurring. Your eventual death, however, is a certainty.

3. Ironically, though your death is inevitable, having life insurance is not always a necessity. With the outcome—your death—predetermined, it is only your situation in life that dictates whether you need life insurance and, if you do, what kind and how much.

One from Column A...

There are so many different types of life insurance that when you put them all down on paper, it begins to look a little like a Chinese menu. In addition to the main courses, there are all kinds of side dishes—riders and special features—that you can order. The worksheets and exercises included later on in this chapter will help you determine if you're a candidate for life insurance and, if so, how much you need. But before you do any of that, take a look at your options.

Despite the many offerings, all life insurance falls into just two categories: term insurance and cash value insurance.

- *Term insurance policies* insure your life for a specific time period—or term— for a specific amount of money, the death benefit. For example, if you purchase a ten-year term life policy for $200,000, and you die within that ten-year period, your beneficiaries will receive $200,000. Period.

- *Cash value insurance* provides a death benefit coupled with a savings or investment plan. Whole life, universal life, and annuities fall into this category. We'll show you how this works later in the chapter.

Term Insurance

The least expensive and purest insurance, term insurance policies are the best kind of insurance to get if all you're interested in is providing an income for your loved ones when you die. Term insurance policies are often favored by young families with modest incomes but large insurance needs. A term insurance policy would be a good choice for a couple in their mid-thirties with three children under the age of ten. A term policy covers a period of time—the term—for which you are insured. At 37 years old, you might want a policy that covers you until you reach age 65. Thus, you would get a 28-year term policy.

You buy coverage in increments of $1,000. You pay the insurance company an annual premium and it pays your beneficiary if you die during the term—the period of time you are insured. If you don't die by the end of the term you don't receive a refund; the insurance company keeps all your premiums. Once your term policy expires you cannot renew it, unless you have been paying for that option. You can, however, purchase another term policy, but it will cost a lot more than the original one because you are older and therefore more likely to die before the new policy expires. So make sure you cover yourself for a long enough period of time the first time.

The two major issues to consider with term life insurance are whether the premiums and death benefits change, and by how much.

Term Insurance and Premiums

There are two basic flavors of term insurance when it comes to premiums:

SINGLE WITH CHILDREN

Minors can't collect insurance benefits. So, if you are single with children, you need to appoint a trustee to administer the proceeds from the life insurance policy if you die. Pick a friend or relative. You may also want the trustee duties to be shared with a bank or financial adviser just in case your trusted choice turns out to be incompetent or untrustworthy when it comes to managing the money for your children.

1. Insurance with annual renewable term and changing premiums.

2. Insurance with level premiums, or premiums that don't change.

Annual Renewable Life Insurance

With this type of insurance, the insurance company absolutely must renew your policy every year. In exchange, your premiums increase over time. This is very attractive, particularly if you are in your early years, because the premiums are small in the beginning—when presumably you have lots of financial obligations and not a lot of money saved to cover those obligations. The premiums rise as you grow older because the likelihood of your death also increases over time, and thus the likelihood that the insurance company will have to pay also increases.

DEATH AND TAXES

While your death is certain, taxes on the proceeds from your life insurance policy are not. Generally, the death benefit of your life insurance policy is not taxable. The proceeds from your insurance policy, however, may be considered part of your estate for tax purposes. Therefore, if your estate is worth more than $600,000, your beneficiary may owe some federal estate tax.

Make sure to check how much the premiums will rise year by year on an annual renewal policy. Some insurance companies try to be tricky. They offer an annual renewal life insurance policy that has extremely low premiums in the first year or two, but then those premiums zoom to astronomical heights. Ask the agent to show you exactly how much you must pay every year of the policy, if you renew each year.

Level Premium Policies

With this type of insurance, the premiums remain constant year after year. It's a trade-off because although in the early years, the premiums for level premium policies are higher than the premiums for annual renewable insurance, in the later years they're lower than annual renewable insurance. For example, if you purchase an annual renewable policy with premiums that start at $350 per year and go up $25 each year for 15 years, the premium the first year is $350, but by the tenth year, it's $600. If you had purchased a level premium policy, your premium might have started at $500 a year, but it would have stayed at that level. You pay more up front with level premium policies, but after 15 years, your premiums will be less than annual renewable premiums.

The most important thing to look for with a level premium policy is the ability to purchase another life insurance policy when your term expires. Also investigate the conditions you must meet in order to renew. For example, some policies let you renew with another level premium policy, but only if you take a physical. If a serious illness is discovered, you may have to pay a whopping new premium to get the policy renewed, if the insurance company will renew at all. Other policies will let you switch to an annual renewable policy or a cash value policy. Check the details.

Term Insurance and Death Benefits

Term insurance can also be subdivided into categories that are distinguished by how the death benefits change. Here, there are three varieties.

1. *Level term insurance* provides a constant amount of insurance for a specified period of time. For example, you might buy a policy for $100,000 that covers you for a ten-year period. So, if you die any time during that ten years, your beneficiaries receive $100,000.

2. *Decreasing term insurance* pays your beneficiaries a decreasing amount of money over the term of the policy. Your premiums decrease in tandem with the decreasing payout. You can buy a decreasing term policy that links your outstanding mortgage obligation to your life insurance policy. The value of the policy decreases in line with the amount due on your mortgage. For example, if you have a 25-year mortgage with another 23 years before it's paid off, you can buy a 23-year term policy that would provide a death benefit that would change each year to match the amount of your outstanding mortgage. Your premiums would also decrease each year in proportion with the decreasing benefit. Decreasing term insurance can also help pay for those hefty college education bills you may face. Let's say you have three teenagers who need to be financed through college

over the next 15 years. You can purchase a decreasing term policy that reflects the decreasing financial obligations you will have for these three children. After they have all graduated from college, you will need less insurance because your children will be forging ahead with their own lives and will be responsible for their own financial well-being.

3. *Increasing term insurance* provides an increasing death benefit over the term of the policy. In this case, your premiums will increase in tandem with the increasing payout. This is an option for a couple with very young children and increasing financial obligations—such as private school and college education.

You can attach a number of different bells and whistles—known as options or riders—to a term policy. You might consider the automatic right to renew the policy up to a certain age, no matter what happens to your health. Two other popular options are the right to convert your policy to whole life insurance and the "waiver of premium" which provides that your insurance will continue—with no further payments from you—if you are disabled.

Cash Value Policies

Cash value policies are life insurance policies that do double duty as investment vehicles. They are much more expensive than term insurance policies and they work like this. Each year, some of the value of your premiums goes into an investment-type account. If you cancel the policy before you die, you will collect that money. Let the money build up, and you may be able to use it in your later years to pay your premiums. You also may be able to borrow against it, and you don't need to repay the loan. The amount you borrowed, however, will be deducted from the payment to your beneficiaries.

A word of caution about the investment aspects of cash value insurance: You really need to concentrate on what the policy does for your family if you die, rather than on how much money you can make on the investment. There are lots of investment vehicles out there that may earn you better rates of return, like stocks, bonds, mutual funds, or even bank certificates of deposit. Cash value policies include:

Whole Life (a.k.a. Permanent Life) Insurance

Whole life covers you for your entire life—as long as you pay the premiums—without the hassles of renewing. The premiums remain constant although the younger you are when you first buy the insurance, the less you will pay each year. Still, you will be overpaying in your early years and underpaying in your later years, since the odds of dying are lower in your younger years than in your older years—the premiums, however, remain the same throughout your life. This is very similar to the payment schedules that electric companies offer, where you pay a constant monthly rate based on your yearly use of electricity. Even if you use more electricity in the summer for that air conditioner than you use in the winter for your heat, your monthly bill is the same month after month. Thus, you overpay actual costs in the winter and underpay the actual costs for the summer.

Limited Payment Life Insurance

Limited payment lets you pay for a specific number of years, after which your policy is "paid up." You make no additional payments, but your beneficiaries still will receive payment upon your death. This type of policy usually is quite expensive since you only pay for the insurance over a limited number of years, but get the coverage for life.

Take a look at how this differs from a 20-year term policy. In a term policy, you pay your annual premium every year for 20 years. If you're still alive after these 20 years, your policy expires, and you must buy a new policy if you still want life insurance. But the story is very different if you have cash value life insurance with a 20-year limited

DIVORCED WITH CHILDREN

You need some life insurance on your ex-spouse as well as yourself if you have custody of your children and are receiving alimony or support payments. Life insurance will guarantee that this income will continue if your ex-spouse dies. If you rely on this money, consider taking out a policy on your ex even if you have to pay for it yourself. Remember, though, your ex-spouse has to know about and agree to this insurance. You can't insure someone else's life without them knowing about it. Of course, if you receive nothing from your ex, you need not open communications on this front.

payment option. The drawback is that you'll pay much higher premiums over the 20-year period than you would with a term policy. The good news is that after 20 years, you pay no more premiums—but your beneficiaries still collect when you die.

Endowment Policies

These are more expensive than whole life policies, but they let you pay up early and also let you collect the face value of your policy even if you are alive. Think of this as whole life with an early payment option—an option for which you must pay a hefty extra price.

Universal Life Insurance

This cash value insurance policy is like a combination plate, tasting a little like term insurance and a little like whole life. It's structured like term insurance, but it costs a little more. The extra money you pay is put in an investment account that earns you a variable rate (with a guaranteed minimum) depending on the performance of the insurance company's investments. Other features include the ability to change the death benefit and premiums or borrow from the account.

Universal Variable Life

Universal variable looks even more like an investment savings plan than an insurance policy. With these policies, you decide how your money will be invested, as opposed to letting the insurance company invest it for you. People who consider themselves experts at investing love this type of policy. The insurance companies offer this type of insurance because they fear that if this option weren't available, these amateur investors might put their money into stocks, bonds, and mutual funds, rather than into insurance.

Living Benefits Insurance

This is a relatively new form of cash value insurance that lets you collect the death benefit while you are still living. It's designed for people who find themselves with

terminal diseases such as AIDS or cancer that require expensive treatment, and it serves to ease the pain and enable patients to spend their final days in as much comfort as possible.

Usually, if you take advantage of the living benefits option, you'll only collect 80 to 90 percent of the total value of your cash value policy at the time you start tapping the policy. Moreover, if you begin receiving benefits when you are still alive, your beneficiaries may not be able to collect any benefits when you die.

Not all policies offer a living benefits option. If your policy does have this option, then if you are diagnosed with a terminal disease you can decide to exercise this option by increasing your premium in order to receive benefits while you are still alive. But if your policy doesn't offer this option, and you're diagnosed with such a disease, you will have a difficult time purchasing a new insurance policy. So plan ahead—if you think it's likely that you may need living benefits insurance, then buy a policy that offers it.

Annuities

Annuities act like pure investment savings animals, with a little bit of life insurance thrown in for spice. They are very popular among people 50 years and older.

You can buy an annuity by putting down a big chunk of money, or you can spread your payments over time. There are two basic types of annuities: fixed and variable. With a fixed annuity, you give the insurance company your money, and they guarantee to pay you a fixed amount of interest on the money you give them. Thus, it doesn't matter to you how well or how poorly the insurance company invests that money, because you'll receive the same payment no matter what.

On the other hand, with a variable rate annuity, you tell the insurance company how you want your money invested from among a number of offerings, such as stocks, bonds, and money market accounts. Your return isn't guaranteed, but rather rests on the fortunes of the investments you've chosen. The smarter you are at investing, the more money you'll reap.

In a sense, the variable rate annuity is the insurance industry's version of an investment account with a stockbroker. The insurance industry doesn't just want your insurance dollars—they'd also love to get your investment dollars. Thus, they offer this investment product, the variable rate annuity.

The important thing to remember about annuities, though, is while you pay all or some money in the beginning, you must wait a certain amount of time before you can begin collecting any payments, unless yours is an immediate annuity.

For example, if you withdraw your money too soon, there could be penalties from the company or the government. Or if you die soon after you invest in an annuity, there might not be enough money built up to take care of the immediate needs of your family. If you're looking for a way to take care of the immediate financial needs of your family if you die, this is not a great deal.

Do You Need Life Insurance?

Now that you've got an overview of the different types of insurance, let's see if you need it.

Singles

Life insurance for single people without dependents often is not necessary. Take a look at Maggie—32 years old, not married, no kids.

A freelance graphic arts designer, Maggie creates Web sites for companies from a one-bedroom condominium she bought five years ago for $75,000. In the past five years, its market value has increased to $87,000. Maggie's debts—not including the mortgage—are limited to the $1,345 combined balance she owes on her MasterCard and Visa.

Maggie is the perfect example of a person who does not need life insurance. What she does need is a last will and testament to make sure that the equity she has in her condominium is passed to whomever she designates.

Of course, if you're single and have a lot of debts but few or no assets, you may want a very small policy to pay those debts and to cover your funeral costs. You probably

don't want to saddle family members with those "final expenses," which is the euphemism insurance salespeople prefer.

Married, No Kids

If you're married, but don't have any kids, you probably need some kind of life insurance. In order to decide how much and what kind, it's necessary to have a talk with your spouse about life after death—his-and-hers style. These conversations are not pleasant, but they really are necessary in order to pinpoint each of your financial needs. The point of life insurance, after all, is to plan for the horrible, possibly unexpected—but also inevitable—fact of death. And it's important to think about it now—not when you're approaching old age—because death can happen at any time. While it won't erase the emotional pain, life insurance will alleviate the financial stress.

TAKE DOUBLE INDEMNITY IF IT DOESN'T COST TWICE AS MUCH

The "double indemnity" option pays twice the amount of insurance you hold in the case of death by accident or violence. Consider taking this option only if it doesn't cost an arm and a leg. Sometimes the premiums aren't that much more—and it might be worth the gamble to your beneficiaries.

For example, let's say you and your spouse are both employed, bringing in fairly equal incomes, have similar expenses, and have incurred similar debt levels. If you died, your daily living costs—for clothes, transportation, food, and such—would be eliminated. But your spouse still would have to pay off the debts you've incurred. How much would it take to do that?

When it comes to rent or a mortgage, two definitely can live cheaper than one. If you pass away and your spouse decides to stay on in the house you purchased together, will he be able to afford the mortgage on his own? If not, you need to take steps to protect him now so that he doesn't lose the house *and* you.

The need for a hefty life insurance policy also exists if your spouse is still going to school and has little or no income. A disabled spouse or one who suffers from a medical condition that hinders employment may also need the steady stream of money that would flow from an insurance policy on your life.

Married with Children

Life insurance is a necessity if you are married with children. Here are some of the things life insurance can help pay for:

1. Families need life insurance on the main breadwinner—either Mom or Dad or both—so that if one dies, the insurance can make up for the lost income.

2. Life insurance can pay for future expenses—like college—as well as current ones.

3. Those "final expenses" are indeed expensive. Life insurance will take care of them.

4. It's a good idea to have enough insurance to pay off most of your debts—perhaps even your mortgage. Your spouse will be dealing first and foremost with the emotional devastation of your death. Life insurance can relieve your spouse from the burden of worrying about making the payment on the auto loan or the mortgage.

5. The spouse who stays home taking care of the kids should have a life insurance policy that is as big as the one you have for the spouse who makes most of the money. If the primary caregiver dies, you may need to hire an outside caregiver, a huge expense that will last until the children are well into adolescent years. And if you do a lot of business traveling, you might need to consider live-in help even for the teens. A life insurance policy will help you pay for all this.

Your particular situation may require additional considerations. It's impossible to cover every possible scenario, but take some time to think about the issues that are important to you before you sign on the dotted line, and be sure you've covered as many bases as you can.

Before You Spend a Cent on Life Insurance

Before you buy any life insurance of your own, check to see if your employer offers a relatively inexpensive policy. The disadvantage to this is that you have to leave your

life insurance behind if you leave your job, but it still may be worth it. Just think of all the money you'll be saving on the premiums until you leave the job.

If employer-sponsored life insurance is not an option, then it's time to do some research on your situation. Use the worksheets on the next few pages to calculate how much life insurance you need before you even talk to an agent. The more they sell, the more money they make in commissions—so be sure you know exactly what your requirements are.

Uncle Sam Can Help, Too

Social Security provides life insurance benefits as well as administering the retirement program. If you die, these members of your family may be eligible to collect Social Security:

* Your spouse, who takes care of a child younger than 16 years old

* Your unmarried children younger than 18 years old, or younger than 19 years if attending elementary or secondary school full time

* Your severely disabled adult child, if the disability started before the child was 22 years old

In 1996, if you died at age 35, your spouse and two children could collect $1,801 a month, if you earned enough quarterly credits and $40,000 the year before. Although it's not enough to maintain a luxury lifestyle, it can certainly help round out your life insurance plan.

How Much Life Insurance Do You Need?

Get out some paper, a pencil, and your calculator. You'll need them to compute how much insurance you need. It's simple to do, but you need to approach this one step at a time. Use the worksheets on pages 176 to 178 to help you determine the amount of life insurance that's right for you.

If You Are H.I.V.-Positive...

...or have some other chronic disease, and you've been denied life insurance, you may be heartened to know that there is at least one company that specializes in high-risk policies. Guarantee Trust Life Insurance of Glenview, IL, has been offering Easy Plan policies—life insurance to organ recipients and people with cancer, diabetes, and coronary disease—and has recently become the first life insurance company to extend coverage to people diagnosed as H.I.V.-positive.

The policies, which provide coverage of up to $250,000 to people who are H.I.V.-positive, cost $1,500 a month. A $50,000 policy costs $300 a month. This compares with $55 a month for a 30-year-old healthy nonsmoker.

For more information, contact:

Guarantee Trust Life Insurance
1275 Milwaukee Ave.
Glenview, IL 60025
(847) 699-0600

The first two columns on the worksheet show how Sara and Bill Dodd—a married couple with four children—would fill out the worksheets. The next two columns are for you (and your spouse, if you have one).

Here's the Dodds' story. They have three children in elementary school and one still toddling at home. Bill runs a computer consulting business—he debugs computer systems for his small business customers—from his home and earns $35,000 a year after expenses. Sara draws a salary of $40,000 as a market analyst with a pharmaceutical firm. They pay a babysitter who watches the school-age kids when they come home and the toddler during the day.

How much insurance do Sara and Bill need? They are each considering $250,000 policies. Let's see if that works.

1. *Current family living expenses:*
   The first thing they do is tally their current annual expenses. Sara needs to calculate how much she spends for housing, food, clothing, medical expenses, and so on, eliminating Bill's portion of those expenses, but including the children's expenses. And Bill needs to do the same thing, eliminating Sara's expenses and adding the children's expenses where applicable. Keep in mind that the categories listed below vary from household to household. You may need to add some as you do your calculations, and of course some will be blank.

CHANGING THE PAYOUT

Life insurance is one of the most varied and flexible insurance products. Although most policies are structured to pay beneficiaries a lump sum, you can buy policies that pay benefits in installments. Ask your agent about the options. If he can't structure the insurance the way you want, consider finding a different agent.

	Bill	Sara	You	Your Spouse
Rent/mortgage	$15,200	$15,200	___	___
Food	7,600	7,600	___	___
Clothing	2,000	3,000	___	___
Utilities	1,500	1,500	___	___
Commuting costs				
Auto maintenance	200	500	___	___
Fuel	1,000	1,000	___	___
Parking	100	100	___	___
Auto loans	0	0	___	___
Other loans	0	0	___	___
Charge cards	1,200	1,500	___	___
Entertainment	1,500	1,500	___	___
Kids' current education	0	0	___	___
Insurance:				
Homeowner's	300	300	___	___
Auto	900	900	___	___
Disability	300	300	___	___
Health	1,000	1,000	___	___
Childcare/eldercare	10,000	10,000	___	___
Kids' lessons	1,000	1,000	___	___
Pension/profit-sharing				
contributions	2,000	2,000	___	___
Taxes	8,700	11,100	___	___
#1 Total	$54,500	$58,500	___	___

2. *Annual income:*

The next step is to add up amounts from all of the income sources to calculate total annual family income.

	Bill	Sara	You	Your Spouse
Wages	$35,000	$40,000	___	___
Social Security benefits	0	0	___	___
Miscellaneous	0	0	___	___
#2 Total	$35,000	$40,000	___	___

3. Next you subtract #2 Total from #1 Total to get #3 Total, the difference between your current income and your current expenses.

	Bill	Sara	You	Your Spouse
#1	$54,500	$58,500	_____	_____
#2	35,000	40,000	_____	_____
#3 Total	$19,500	$18,500	_____	_____

4. Now estimate the cost of sending the kids to college.

	Bill	Sara	You	Your Spouse
#4 Kids' educations	$200,000	$200,000	_____	_____

5. Estimate estate settlement costs.

	Bill	Sara	You	Your Spouse
Funeral expenses	$4,500	$4,500	_____	_____
Uninsured medical costs	500	500	_____	_____
#5 Total	$5,000	$5,000	_____	_____

If your spouse was ill prior to dying, you'll have to pay those medical bills that your spouse's health insurance did not. Be sure to include this—which at the very least equals the applicable deductibles—in the calculations.

6. Next add #4 Total to #5 Total to get #6, the total future expenses.

	Bill	Sara	You	Your Spouse
#4	$200,000	$200,000	_____	_____
#5	5,000	5,000	_____	_____
#6 Total	$205,000	$205,000	_____	_____

7. Multiply the figure you calculated in step 3, by 10.

	Bill	Sara	You	Your Spouse
#3	$ 19,500	$ 18,500	_____	_____
Multiplied by 10	10	10	_____	_____
#7 Total	$195,000	$185,000	_____	_____

8. Now add the total future expenses (#6) to #7 Total.

	Bill	Sara	You	Your Spouse
#7	$195,000	$185,000	_____	_____
#6	205,000	205,000	_____	_____
#8 Total	$400,000	$390,000	_____	_____

These are your total expenses for the next ten years.

9. List your assets.

	Bill	Sara	You	Your Spouse
Emergency fund	$15,000	$15,000	_____	_____
Investment income	5,000	5,000	_____	_____
Rental income	0	0	_____	_____
Other	0	0	_____	_____
Cash/savings accounts	30,000	30,000	_____	_____
Employer life insurance	0	120,000	_____	_____
#9 Total	$50,000	$170,000	_____	_____

Don't include pension plan money or 401(k) and IRA investments. These funds are for your retirement. Besides, they are not available to you unless you want to pay a huge tax penalty. Do include any money set aside for your children's college education. Even though you think of these funds as earmarked for the kids, they are part of the total assets from which your family can draw.

10. To get the final figure for your life insurance needs, subtract #9 Total (assets) from #8 Total (expenses) to get #10 (life insurance needs).

	Bill	Sara	You	Your Spouse
#8	$400,000	$390,000	_____	_____
#9	50,000	170,000	_____	_____
#10 Total	$350,000	$220,000	_____	_____

So let's take a look at this #10 Total for Bill and Sara—their life insurance needs. As you can see, Sara's worksheet includes one big asset that Bill's does not. Through her employer, Sara carries life insurance equal to three times her salary for a total of $120,000. After filling out their worksheets, Sara discovers she needs $220,000

worth of additional life insurance. Bill finds he will need $350,000 to insure his life. The $250,000 policies each was considering purchasing would have been a mistake: For Sara, it would have been too much, and for Bill, too little.

What Kind of Insurance for Sara and Bill?

The best type of insurance for Sara and Bill is term insurance. It's less expensive and answers the insurance question: How do we provide financial security for our family if one of us dies?

For them, a term policy with an annual renewal option is preferable to a level premium because they may want to change the amount of insurance they have from time to time. Bill's income might grow faster than Sara's. Their expenses may significantly increase should they sell their home and buy a larger, more expensive house. Of course, their assets may grow, too, if Bill's mother dies and leaves Bill and his brother her estate worth $750,000. Thus, they may have to raise or lower the insurance each carries, depending on life's changes. They might also consider buying a separate term policy that pays decreasing benefits so that their mortgage obligation is covered if either dies.

You, too, need to evaluate your life insurance needs every year. Your marital status could change. You might go from a salaried job with a life insurance policy as part of the benefit package to a freelance business. Whatever the changes, you need to adjust the amount, and perhaps type, of life insurance you buy to reflect the financial impact of your death on those you care for.

Remember, your life insurance is not a measure of the value of your life. It does reflect, though, the financial assets your family would need in the event that you died.

Shopping for Life Insurance

Once you determine how much insurance you need and the type you want, shopping for the least expensive policy is not difficult at all. Remember that understanding the insurance company's motivations for selling you specific types of insurance makes it easier to do your shopping with confidence. Life insurance is a gamble just like every

other type of insurance. With term insurance, it's obvious. The insurance company is betting that you won't die before the term is up. So, the more people who buy term insurance, the more their risk is spread.

Cash policies are a little different though. Insurance companies are destined to pay out on a cash policy. But then again, the premiums are much higher, so the company has already factored in the added risk of selling cash policies when calculating the premiums you have to pay. They get more of your money up front than if they sell you a term policy, and even though they're eventually going to have to pay out, they will have invested your money and made a tidy sum for themselves. Ideally (for them), they'll end up only having to pay you a small fraction of what you've paid them.

Before you meet with any agents, understand your own needs and insurance goals. While a good agent can help you develop your policy just like a good financial planner, another may influence you to buy something that you may not need.

If you need term life insurance, or just want to see how the premiums you are paying compare with what other term policies cost, there are a number of quote services available that you can call for free. These quote services are merely agencies that sell insurance for lots of different companies. They provide you with quotes from all the insurance companies they represent. To make these quote compilations look unbiased, they sometimes throw in quotes from companies that they don't represent and that have higher premiums than the ones they do represent. Still, you have nothing to lose by getting quotes from these services, since they're free.

When you call, tell the quote service how much term insurance you want and the type of term insurance you want, including any riders or options. These quote firms then search through the offerings of a number of different insurance companies and provide you with free quotes. The quote services hope you will buy an insurance policy through them, but you are in no way obligated to do so.

Most quote services offer both telephone and Internet access. Here's a listing of some that operate nationwide:

InsuranceQuote
(800) 972-1104
http://www.iquote.com

MasterQuote of America
(800) 627-5433
http://www.masterquote.com

Quotesmith
(800) 556-9393
http://www.quotesmith.com

Selectquote
(800) 289-5807
http://www.selectquote.com

TermQuote
(800) 444-8376
http://www.rcinet.com/~termquote

Another quote service alternative is Information Insurance at (800) 808-5810. This service does charge $50, but it surveys some 600 companies compared to the one or two dozen the other quote services cover. And Information Insurance promises to get you the lowest quotes available or it will refund your $50.

Whether you are looking for term or cash value insurance, you can always call an insurance agent listed in the yellow pages. Better still, get friends and relatives to recommend agents they have worked with and liked.

A more expensive alternative is to hire a financial adviser to help you sort through the various policies, particularly if you are considering a cash value policy. This can cost anywhere from $75 to $200 an hour. Do remember, you will be paying not only the adviser but also some type of up-front sales charge associated with the policy. That's two charges before even a nickel of your insurance money is applied to the premium. Spending a little time to do the research yourself means more money in your pocket and less in someone else's.

Check It Out

You are ready for the final step on the road to getting the right life insurance at the best price. You need to check out the health of the insurance company or companies you are considering.

This is absolutely necessary because you do not want your family to be left trying to collect death benefits from a company that is unable to pay because it is financially dead or dying. You don't want to have to rely on the state-operated programs that step in to pay your beneficiaries if the insurance company from which you bought your life insurance has gone bankrupt. These state programs will make good on policies issued by companies that die before you do, but your beneficiaries may have to wait many months to get the money due to them. Meanwhile, how will the mortgage payment be made? How will the utility bills be paid? What about the car payments?

Contact the rating services listed on page 211. Look for insurance companies with some type of "A" rating. The higher the rating the better when it comes to life insurance companies.

Now you are ready to buy the policy you want. One good thing about buying life insurance is that most life insurance companies are required by law to give you a ten-day grace period. During this time, if you've signed a contract for life insurance but decide you want to back out of the policy, you can do so—without any penalty. The contract is canceled, and you get back that first premium.

Of course, if you've followed the step-by-step process just outlined, you won't have second thoughts. You will know you've got the right amount and type of insurance with a financially robust firm, and at a decent price.

THE WEIRD, the *stupid,* and the WRONG

CHAPTER THIRTEEN

Protect yourself from people who want to sell you worthless or useless insurance. Policies such as these are just tacky, poorly made doodads that obscure the solid design of the total insurance structure you have built for yourself. Learn what to avoid to keep your insurance plan clear of costly but useless items.

Your total insurance structure is now in place. The floors—your health insurance—are secure and even reinforced with your disability insurance. Your walls—residential and auto insurance—are steady and firm. If you need it, you've capped it with a ceiling of life insurance.

Now, you just need to make sure that structure does not get overloaded with insurance you don't need. You work hard for your money. There's no reason to part with it for insurance that's weird or stupid. And you do need to make sure you don't get taken by scam operators.

Remember, insurance companies and agents make money selling you insurance whether you need it or not. The companies and agents can supply you with information and offer options. You, though, are the one who is responsible for evaluating those options and picking the insurance that meets your needs at the best possible price.

Generally, insurance policies that cover very narrow or time- or event-specific situations are bad deals. Take a look at the rundown of special insurance and why, in most instances, it's wise to pass it up.

Of course, if any of these types of insurance described in this chapter show up in a benefits package that your employer offers you, and you don't have to pay for them, accept them graciously and say thanks. But if you have to pay for these yourself with your hard-earned dollars, it's probably a good idea to pass.

Credit Card Insurance

If you have a checking account or own a credit card, you've probably been solicited to purchase one of two types of credit card insurance. Don't buy it. Here's why.

The first type of insurance covers you for lost or stolen credit cards. In exchange for an annual fee—usually $35—the company will cover any charges over $50 that somebody else places on your card. Sounds like a good deal? It isn't, for two reasons:

1. Your homeowner's policy probably covers this kind of a loss.

2. Credit card companies already limit your liability to $50 if you report the lost or stolen card immediately.

The second type of credit card insurance involves registering your credit cards with a company that you then call if your cards are stolen or lost. The company, in turn, calls all your credit card companies and notifies them to cancel your cards. This is not insurance at all. It is a service.

Parody Policies

To qualify for UFO abduction, reincarnation, and a slew of other faux insurance policies, prospective buyers must pass a humor test from Mike St. Lawrence. Formerly employed in the insurance industry, St. Lawrence now makes his living by selling parody policies which poke fun at the serious posture that industry representatives frequently assume when trying to make a buck by selling you insurance you may not need.

Humor, not insurance coverage, is the aim of these policies. To make sure that consumers are not misled, St. Lawrence imposes the humor qualifying test. "If you answer 'yes' to more than one of the questions, you don't qualify," says St. Lawrence. Here's the test:

- Do you have a sense of humor?

- Do you take this insurance seriously?

- Were your parents related before they were married?

All the parody policies are for $10 million. Benefits are paid in equal installments of $1 a year for 10 million years. The UFO abduction policy provides "double indemnity coverage if the aliens insist on conjugal visits or if the aliens refer to the abductee as a nutritional food source or 'the other white meat,' " says St. Lawrence.

You can order one of the many policies St. Lawrence offers from:

The St. Lawrence Agency
319 The Hermit's Trail
Altamont Springs, FL 32701
(800) 728-5413
Web site: http://www.ufo2001.com

How much are you willing to pay to make one call rather than ten? Fifty dollars? Seventy-five? The smart answer is zero. Instead, just make sure you have a list of your credit cards and credit card company phone numbers. You'll probably be able to complete the calls within an hour. If your purse or wallet is stolen, the big hassle is not calling the credit card companies. It involves canceling your checking account and getting a new one and, of course, waiting in line to get a new driver's license.

Travel Insurance

Travel insurance comes in lots of different forms, which means there are lots of different kinds of insurance you probably don't need. Take a look.

Trip Cancellation Insurance

This insurance provides coverage if you have to cancel your trip due to illness, a death in the immediate family, or some other calamity. The important thing in evaluating these policies is to clearly understand what situations activate the insurance. That's because if a situation is not specifically stated, it is not covered. These policies usually reimburse you for the unused portion of your trip if you or an immediate family member becomes ill or injured during the trip.

It's expensive insurance for what you get. The cost is generally 5 to 7 percent of the price of the vacation. The odds are generally low that a major illness or family catastrophe will strike when you are on vacation. And this insurance does not cover any medical costs for that illness or for the new ticket you'll need to purchase to fly you home if that emergency summons you after you're on the slopes or basking on the beach.

It's very disappointing to have to cancel a vacation, but it may not be a risk worth insuring. Losing the $2,000 you spent on airline tickets to Colorado is an inconvenience, not a disaster. There are, however, specific types of travel insurance policies that are worth considering. You might want to consider insuring that once-in-a-lifetime trip around the world, or a $20,000 honeymoon to Australia.

Beware of Twisting

Twisting happens when insurance agents persuade clients to cash in old policies to purchase new, more expensive ones, whether the customers need them or not. The person who needs these new policies is actually the agent, who racks up higher commissions every time a new policy is sold. Twisting is illegal, and victims of twisting have successfully sued insurers caught doing it to the tune of over $400 million this year alone.

Robert Morris is an elderly Indiana resident who may have been a victim of a huge twisting scheme during the 1980s. He claims his agent persuaded him to convert whole life insurance policies that paid over $6.4 million in death benefits to universal life policies with over $10.1 million in benefits. Although on first inspection the deal looked like a good one—not only did the death benefits almost double, loans from the cash value of the new policies were to be used to pay the premiums—Morris contends the agent did not explain that this was contingent on continued rising interest rates.

When the interest rates began to fall in the mid-1980s, the insurance companies began to bill Morris for hundreds of thousands of dollars in premiums. Morris paid the bills until 1995 when he decided to sue his insurer for reimbursement of the premiums plus interest. As of May 1997 the case had not yet been settled.

Cancellation Waivers

Waivers are offered by some tour or cruise operators for a fee that ranges from $40 to $60. This is not insurance. Like trip cancellation insurance, waivers provide coverage if you have to cancel a trip, but they have loads of restrictions that make it difficult for you to collect, the worst of which is you may not be able to get reimbursed if your tour operator gets into financial difficulty. This type of insurance isn't regulated by the state departments of insurance, so if your tour company goes under, your deposit will probably go under with it. What's more, they will not cover you all the way up to the last minute before departure, which is usually when most people need to cancel their trip.

Baggage Insurance

This insurance is aptly named because it's nothing but baggage for you and profit for someone else. To insure $1,000 worth of your personal belongings for a week would typically cost $50. Often, this insurance is offered by tour operators. Don't buy it. You're probably already covered.

The U.S. Department of Transportation requires airlines to be liable for checked bag losses of up to $1,250 for each traveler on domestic flights. If you're traveling on an international flight, check to see what your airline covers.

It's also a good idea to consult your homeowner's policy, which may cover off-premises theft or loss. If you are traveling with expensive electronic equipment, jewelry, or sporting gear, it probably is more cost effective to purchase a floater or endorsement to your homeowner's policy to cover these items. The cost to insure a $1,000 ring could range from $10 to $40. This would provide full coverage for the ring, anywhere in the world you travel, and it usually covers the item for one full year whether you are on a trip or not.

Emergency Medical Assistance

These policies would cover you if you had to be airlifted off a mountain due to a skiing or hiking accident or had to stay for a prolonged period of time in a foreign hospital. It also provides coverage if you get seriously ill or injured and need to be flown home.

Health Insurance for Your Pet

Nancy Van der Wel of Seattle saw a brochure about pet health insurance in her vet's office a few years ago. She bought a policy to cover her yellow Labrador retriever that cost her about $100 a year. When Samantha was diagnosed with Addison's disease, an ailment that affects the adrenal glands and costs about $1,800 to treat, Van der Wel turned to her pet insurance to help pay for it. She was only able to collect $1,000 and decided to stop the coverage when the dog's expenses exceeded the policy's limit.

If you're considering pet health insurance, consider this:

• Most policies don't cover routine office visits.

• Most veterinary bills cost less than the deductibles.

• Most policies don't cover pre-existing conditions.

• It's difficult to get coverage for elderly pets, whose owners need it the most.

Get Smart

Here are three basic rules of thumb for avoiding scams and useless insurance.

1. Never buy a policy if you feel pressured by the agent, particularly if she tells you that you must make a decision immediately. No reputable agent will do that. If you are confronted by someone who is pressuring you, just tell that person to go away. If the calls persist, contact your state department of insurance and report the offender.

2. Never, ever write out a check to an agent. Always write the check to the insurance company. Again, no reputable agent should even take a check unless it is written to the company providing the insurance.

3. Never deal with an agent who refuses to answer—or just plain can't answer—your questions. Of course, your agent may not know every answer on the spot to every question you ask. "I don't know, but I'll get back to you later" is a perfectly fine response. But do make sure you get a reply quickly. An agent who doesn't return your phone calls within 24 hours will probably be impossible to reach when you need to file a claim in response to an emergency.

Do be wary, though, of an agent who gives the "I-don't-know-but..." response to too many of your questions. That may indicate a lack of knowledge about the policy. No matter how nice that person may seem, you need an agent who's fully informed about the policy you're buying, as well as other options that might work better for you. This is probably a good time to contact another agent.

Not only are these possibilities as remote as the Himalayan mountain you are considering scaling, but the coverage may be unnecessary. Check what your health insurance covers for out-of-the-country trips. Most cover the standard charges for any necessary medical care you receive. That's true, as well, if you belong to an HMO.

Before you travel out of the country, ask your health insurer for any paperwork that foreign medical providers might have to fill out in order for you to be covered. If you get sick, ask the medical providers to complete the forms while you are still in their care. After you return to the United States, you don't want to have to track down the hospital in northern Thailand that set your broken leg.

Medigap policies C through J cover foreign medical care and they make good sense for seniors who travel outside the United States. These policies provide 80 percent coverage of the costs for necessary care after a $250 deductible. Be aware, though, that they cover only the first 60 days of a trip.

Legal Insurance

About a decade ago, the concept of legal insurance got a lot of press coverage. Since then, it hasn't progressed much. That's good news because if you have to pay a lot for it, you probably don't need it. There are two basic types of legal insurance:

1. Plans that charge a yearly fee in exchange for the services of a lawyer for such personal matters as drawing up a will, or handling a real estate closing, bankruptcy, or an uncontested divorce

2. Plans that charge a discounted hourly rate for a lawyer's services

Either way, you probably are better off skipping this insurance and paying a lawyer as you might need one. However, if you're offered this type of insurance as a benefit at your job, don't balk. You'll be glad you have it when you ask your lawyer to write that one letter for $250.

Legal insurance covers only the cost of a lawyer, not the cost of the legal liability that necessitated hiring the lawyer. Your legal liability for damage you might do to someone else is already covered by your homeowner's or automobile insurance.

Scams on the Road Paved with Good Intentions

The difference between being a victim of an insurance scam and buying insurance you don't need is merely the intent of the person selling you insurance. Moreover, those differences are not black and white, but shades of gray.

An example of an insurance scam is when a salesperson knows that the so-called insurance is just a means of getting money from you in exchange for something that is worthless. That's pretty clear. The odds of being scammed by professionals of this ilk are really pretty small.

Your big risk comes from the ignorant or greedy person who is convinced that you need insurance when you don't. Every time a travel agent sells you accidental death insurance for an airline flight, you've been taken. Every time you purchase a life insurance policy for a child, you've been taken. Every time an insurance agent lets you renew your collision insurance with coverage for more than your car is worth, you've been taken.

Protect yourself from these well-intentioned but ill-informed so-called professionals. It doesn't matter whether they mean to defraud you or not, you're still paying for something that is useless.

ACCESSING *information* in CYBERSPACE

CHAPTER FOURTEEN

Now that you understand how to build the structure to protect your health, your life, and your property, use the Internet to access lots of information on specific topics. Get information on companies, on quote services, and on how to find an appraiser for that diamond ring you just acquired.

Cyberspace is loaded with information about insurance. Web sites range from the very helpful, to the confusingly esoteric, to the in-your-screen advertisement for a local insurance agency. Sorting through this flotsam and jetsam of data can consume a horrendous amount of time for negligible results.

The great thing about visiting insurance Web sites is that you never have to talk to an insurance agent. Of course, it may take a minute to two for the Web site to appear on

your screen, but at least you don't have to wait on perma-hold or maneuver through the myriad options of voice mail to get the information you want.

To move smoothly through cyberspace, there are four general insurance information Web sites you might want to try:

1. The Insurance Industry Internet Network (http://www.iiin.com) provides information on insurance-related news as well as a list of insurance companies. The Web site provides links to scores of other home pages and is a good starting point for information on just about every type of insurance you are researching.

2. InsWeb Insurance On-Line (http://www.insweb.com) is a similar alternative. Life, health, and auto insurance are covered on this site, and you'll also find a useful FAQ section on homeowner's policies.

3. Insurance News Network (http://www.insure.com) is filled with information about the basics of homeowner's, auto, and life insurance. Here you also can get ratings on the financial health of insurance companies and information concerning insurance firms operating in the state in which you live.

4. The Insurance Information Institute Web site (http://www.iii.org) is another good source for browsers. The information on property and casualty insurance is more complete than on health and life insurance.

Rating Service Companies

You can directly access the Web sites for the rating service companies to get the low-down on the financial health of an insurance company you are considering. Here are the site addresses.

- A. M. Best (http://www.ambest.com)

- Duff & Phelps Credit Rating (http://www.duffllc.com)

- Moody's Investor Service (http://www.moodys.com)

- Standard & Poor's (http://www.ratings.standardpoor.com)

Government Resources

The Social Security Administration (http://www.ssa.gov) has extended its arm onto the Internet. You can get information concerning the retirement, disability, and Medicare programs, and how to apply to collect benefits from Uncle Sam's insurance programs.

The National Asssociation of Insurance Commissioners (http://www.naic.org) operates a Web site that provides you with a listing of each of the state insurance departments as well as links to information about the insurance laws and regulations in each of the 50 states.

Health Insurance

Through its Web site, the National Committee for Quality Assurance (http://www.ncqa.org) lets you look at the quality ratings it has given to HMOs. It also provides a rundown on how it goes about the rating process. Use the various aspects of an HMO it examines as a checklist when you research a local HMO that has not yet been rated by NCQA.

The IRS (http://www.irs.ustreas.gov) provides answers to the 29 most frequently asked questions about Medical Savings Accounts (MSAs).

The Council for Affordable Health Insurance (http://www.cahi.com) provides information about a variety of health insurance topics through its Web site. It's also a good source on Medical Savings Accounts.

Try the home page for the Health Insurance Association of America (http://www.hiaa.org) to access information about health insurance and disability insurance.

The American Association of Health Plans (http://www.aahp.org) specializes in information about HMOs and patient rights. This is a good site to visit if you need information about fair and unfair insurance payments.

Appraisers

If you want to find an appraiser, there are two good Web sites. The American Society of Appraisers (http://www.appraisers.org) can supply you with the name of an appraiser in your local community who can value just about anything, from real estate to personal property items.

The Appraisers Association of America provides appraisers primarily for personal property such as art, antiques, and jewelry. To locate one in your community, you need to go through CompuServe. You can reach them at 102212,3542@ Compuserve.com.

Life Insurance Companies

The Insurance Company yellow pages (http://www.lifecom.com) provides a directory of Web sites for individual life insurance companies. Home pages for individual insurance companies provide a wide range of information. You can get general information about the types of insurance the company offers and listings for the insurance company's agents in your local area. You can even request that someone contact you to supply a rate quote for a specific type of insurance.

WRAPPING *it* UP

CHAPTER FIFTEEN

You've constructed the insurance plan that meets your needs and gives you the best coverage for yourself and those you love. You can rearrange it as your circumstances change, and relax knowing you've built a protective framework to help you deal with the unexpected.

Insurance is about taking control of your life, regardless of what comes up. Everyone's requirements are different, which is why there are all kinds of plans. Putting together a strong yet flexible custom-designed insurance package that works for you requires a game plan.

You evaluate your risks, calculate how much insurance you need and the amount of financial risk you can comfortably assume yourself, and then decide on the price you're willing to pay to transfer the rest of the risk. Finally, you examine your options and choose the policies that safeguard you and those you love.

Changing and Rearranging

As time goes by, you will be reconstructing your plan. Sometimes, these renovations will be minor, such as dropping your collision insurance or adding a rider to your homeowner's policy when you acquire an expensive piece of jewelry. Other times, the changes will be more substantial. For example, your life insurance needs may shift dramatically over the years depending on whether you get married and how many children you have.

Whenever you have a change in your life, think about how it affects your insurance coverage. If you move from the city to the country, for example, your automobile insurance costs may decline because theft is less likely. On the other hand, your homeowner's insurance may increase because the nearest hook-and-ladder may be ten miles away rather than just a few city blocks.

Restructuring in Five Easy Steps

Here's a recap of the five points you need to cover when you change, drop, or add insurance coverage.

1. Assess what your own insurance needs are. You know best what you need. Don't put that decision in the hands of an insurance company or agent.

2. Understand the types of insurance available and the protection they provide. If you move to a flood-plain area, you'll want to check out flood insurance. Or as the value of your car declines you may be able to drop your collision insurance.

3. Become familiar with the different types of provisions within a specific type of insurance.

4. Understand how to compare insurance policies by evaluating the coverage and the premiums. You use different criteria to compare homeowner's policies than you do to examine HMOs. Make sure you understand the critical issues for each type of insurance.

5. Be savvy about insurance companies and salespeople. Make sure the companies are financially sound and provide good service. Demand a level of expertise from agents who are thoroughly familiar with the policies and who respond to your questions quickly.

Risk, Peril, and Hazard Forever

Every time you rejigger your insurance plan, keep in mind these three basic concepts:

1. *Risk* is the chance of loss. Insurance companies view a person or the property insured as the risk, because that person or property could sustain a loss. Your car, your house, and your body are risks.

2. *Peril* is the cause of the loss—an auto accident, a storm, or a slippery floor.

3. *Hazard* increases the likelihood of loss due to a peril. The type of material used to construct your house represents a hazard. A brick home is less likely to be consumed by fire (a peril) than a frame house. But, a brick home is more vulnerable to earthquake (another peril) than a frame home. You can control some hazards and thus decrease the cost of your insurance. For example, if you install burglar and/or fire alarms in your dwelling, you may be eligible for a discount on your homeowner's premiums.

Take Charge

As you update and refine your insurance plan, you will gather information and get input from a host of different sources. Keep in mind that these resources can be valuable resources, but that you are always the boss.

Don't be afraid to ask questions. No query is stupid—but it's very important that you understand the answers. If insurance agents are rude, condescending, or just not there when you have a question, let them know you're prepared to move to another company. There are a lot of insurance companies that compete for your business. You have a right to demand attentive and knowledgeable service.

If you've followed all the steps outlined throughout these chapters, you know you've created a sound overall insurance plan for the right price. You also have the insight to know when to re-evaluate your needs. And finally, you've got the tools to build new insurance configurations to fit those changing needs throughout your life.

You've done a lot of good work here. Now it's time to rest. When your personalized insurance plan is in place, it will reward you with a comforting sense of security—because insurance is all about limiting your risk and giving you peace of mind. You can't anticipate all of life's problems, but your insurance policies will buffer the mishaps and help you manage your future.

GLOSSARY

accelerated benefits: Payments to beneficiaries of some life insurance policies that are distributed before the policyholder dies, due to extenuating circumstances like terminal or chronic illness.

accidental death benefits: Additional payments to beneficiaries of some life insurance policies if the policyholder dies as a result of an accident.

accumulation period: The amount of time during which the holder of an annuity contract pays into the fund.

actual cash value: The replacement cost of property less the value of depreciated property.

actuary: A professional who calculates insurance premiums, risk, dividends, and reserves.

additional living expenses: The cost of food, lodging, and other expenses covered by homeowner's insurance that policyholders incur while their homes are being rebuilt following damage.

adjustable life insurance: A type of insurance that allows for changes in premium payments, protection periods, and the death benefit of the policy.

adjuster: An individual who determines the amount of loss when a claim is submitted.

annual policy: A type of insurance policy that covers a period of one year.

annuitant: The individual who receives the payments of an annuity plan.

annuity: A tax-deferred investment offered by insurance companies that provides for yearly payments or payments at regular intervals.

annuity consideration: The payments made by the holder of an annuity contract.

application: Information you provide to the insurance company when you request coverage.

appraisal: A statement that describes the value of property or assets or the amount of loss or damage.

appurtenant structures: Buildings other than houses covered by homeowner's policies. Examples are garages, toolsheds, and hothouses.

arbitration: A procedure whereby a three-person panel of appraisers settles insurance claim disputes. One appraiser is chosen by the insurance company, one is chosen by the person filing the claim, and the third is chosen by the other two appraisers.

arson: The act of setting fire to property with criminal or fraudulent intent.

assignment: The transfer of an insurance policy to another individual.

assurance: A term used interchangeably with insurance, usually in Great Britain and Canada.

automatic premium loan: An arrangement to use the cash value of a life insurance policy to take out a loan with the purpose of paying premiums that have not been paid by the end of the grace period.

automobile liability insurance: Coverage that protects the policyholder from liability for injuries to others and damage to someone else's property as a result of a car accident.

automobile physical damage insurance: Coverage for damages to a policyholder's car caused by collision, fire, or theft.

beneficiary: An individual (or financial instrument, like a trust fund) who receives payments if the policyholder dies.

benefit: The amount of money paid to you or your beneficiaries for a legitimate claim. A benefit can also take the form of rights, such as the right to renew a policy under favorable conditions, to add extra coverage, or to choose settlement options.

bodily injury liability insurance: Coverage that reimburses others for personal injury or loss of one's car due to collision, fire, theft, or other cause that is the fault of the policyholder.

cancellation: The premature termination of insurance policy.

cash value: The amount of money available to life insurance policyholders.

casualty insurance: [See: liability insurance.]

certificate: A document that details the provisions of an insurance policy.

claim: A request for payment of insurance benefits.

coinsurance: An arrangement in a health insurance policy whereby the insured individual pays a portion of the expenses and the insurance company pays the rest.

collision insurance: Automobile insurance that pays for damages caused by violent impact to your car by another vehicle or object.

commission: A compensation arrangement that provides for a percentage of the premium to be paid to the insurance agent.

comprehensive automobile insurance: Coverage for perils other than collision, including theft, vandalism, fire, windstorms, floods, and other perils.

concealment: Failure to disclose details to the insurance company that might affect your insurance coverage.

conditions: Statements of rights and duties of both parties—the insured individual and the insurance company—to an insurance contract.

condominium insurance: A policy that covers unit owners for personal property and liability separate from the insurance the condo association carries.

Consolidated Omnibus Budget Reconciliation Act of 1985 (COBRA): A law requiring employers to extend your health coverage for up to 18 months after you leave a job.

convertible term insurance: A term life insurance policy that provides the opportunity for the policyholder to exchange it for permanent life insurance without undergoing a physical exam.

cost-of-living rider: A provision of a term life insurance policy that allows for the purchase of additional insurance in increasing amounts (with corresponding increases in death benefits) that are tied to the cost of living.

coverage: The amount of protection provided by an insurance policy.

credit life insurance: A type of term life insurance that is issued through a lender that provides for loan repayment or payment of other obligations in the event the borrower dies.

declaration: A portion of an insurance policy that includes the policyholder's name and address and the policy's terms, effective date, amount, and premium payments.

declination: The rejection of an application for life insurance by an insurance company.

decreasing term life insurance: Term life insurance whose face value decreases over time.

deductible: The amount of money a policyholder pays out before the insurance company pays a claim.

deposit term insurance: A type of term life insurance that requires higher first-year premiums and that usually pays a partial endowment at the end of the term which can be applied to a new policy.

depreciation: The loss of value of property over a period of time.

direct agent: An individual who sells the insurance of only one insurance company.

direct writer: An insurance company that employs salespeople who sell that company's policies exclusively.

disability benefit: A payment from an insurance company to an individual who has become disabled and who has a disability insurance policy. Some life insurance policies also provide for waivers of premium payments if the policyholder becomes permanently disabled.

dividend: Money returned to participating insurance policyholders as a result of a surplus due to decreasing claims or increasing investment returns.

double indemnity policy: A type of life insurance that pays twice the amount of benefits to survivors if the policyholder dies under certain circumstances—usually a type of accident.

endorsement: An addition to a property/casualty insurance policy.

endowment: Benefits paid to the holder of a life insurance policy if the holder is still living at the maturity date, or to the beneficiary if the policyholder dies before the maturity date.

exclusion: The denial of coverage for certain perils, individuals, locations, or property.

exclusive agent: An individual who sells and services insurance policies, works for one company, and is either paid a commission, salary, or a combination of both.

expiration date: The date on which an insurance policy ceases to be in effect.

exposure: Possibility of loss.

face amount: The amount of money to be paid to beneficiaries if the policyholder dies or when the policy matures, exclusive of amounts specified in special provisions.

FAIR plans: Cooperative insurance plans sponsored by state governments that make certain types of insurance accessible that would be otherwise unavailable.

fee-for-service plan: A traditional health insurance plan that involves paying a monthly premium in return for comprehensive medical coverage.

first party: A policyholder.

floater: A type of insurance coverage for movable possessions like art, jewelry, and furs that protects against loss of property, regardless of where the object is lost, stolen, or damaged.

fraud: The intentional concealment or misrepresentation of facts for the purpose of collecting insurance benefits or selling policies.

grace period: The amount of time that an insurance policy remains effective after a premium is missed.

group insurance: A type of insurance obtained through membership to an organization or association or by working for an employer.

guaranteed renewable: A type of insurance that is automatically renewed until the policyholder reaches a predetermined age. The rate can change, but only as it applies to a whole category of individuals.

hazard: A situation that causes property loss, personal injury, or death.

health insurance: Insurance that covers payments for medication or to medical providers and hospitals.

health maintenance organization (HMO): An organization that provides medical coverage through a specific group of hospitals and doctors. There are no deductibles, except for prescriptions.

homeowner's insurance: A type of insurance that includes coverage for loss or damage of property, additional living expenses incurred as a result of property loss or damage, and personal liability.

indemnity: Insurance benefits or reimbursement for loss.

independent agent: An individual who is paid a commission to sell and service insurance policies, and who usually represents more than one company.

insured: Person covered by an insurance policy.

lapsed policy: An insurance policy that is no longer effective due to the nonpayment of premiums after the grace period has ended.

level premium life insurance: A type of life insurance for which you pay premiums that remain the same over the duration of the policy.

liability: An obligation that can be legally enforced.

liability insurance: Tthis type of insurance that provides protection from financial legal obligations. Also known as casualty insurance.

liability limit: The total amount of money for which an insurance company agrees to cover the holder of a liability insurance policy.

maturity: The date on which the insurance company pays the policyholder the endowment portion of that individual's life insurance.

medical savings account: A plan that allows you to make tax-deductible contributions to an account you will use to pay for health coverage.

moral hazard: Risks caused by the behavior of a policyholder, like intentionally setting a fire to collect insurance.

mortality table: A chart that shows death rates for people at different ages.

mortgage insurance: A type of life insurance that pays the remainder of the policyholder's mortgage when the individual dies.

multiline company: A firm that sells different types of insurance, for example home and auto.

mutual insurance companies: Insurance firms that are owned by their policyholders.

named perils: Property insurance coverage for loss from certain situations specifically listed in the policy rather than protection from loss due to any variety of causes.

National Flood Insurance Program (NFIP): Federal government-sponsored insurance that covers the policyholder for property losses caused by floods.

negligence: A failure to exercise a level of care that could result in injury, death, or loss of or damage to property.

no-fault automobile insurance: A type of insurance that covers injuries and losses as a result of a car accident regardless of who caused the accident.

notice of loss: The act of informing an insurance company of a loss.

occupational hazard: Dangers inherent to a job that increase the likelihood of illness, injury, or death.

omnibus clause: A provision in a car insurance policy that covers drivers of the policyholder's car.

ordinary life insurance: Whole, term, and endowment life insurance policies.

package policy: Two or more types of insurance combined into a single policy. A homeowner's policy package might include coverage for property, liability, and theft.

partial disability: An injury or illness that prevents a policyholder from performing part of her job.

peril: The cause of potential injury, death, loss, or damage. Examples of peril are fire, theft, and windstorms.

permanent insurance: A category of life insurance that includes whole life, universal life, variable life, and endowment policies.

personal injury protection automobile insurance (PIP): A type of insurance that covers medical expenses, loss of income, and other expenses that result from a car accident.

personal lines: Insurance policies for individuals and families, as opposed to business insurance.

personal property: Possessions like furniture, art, electronic equipment, or jewelry, which are not permanently attached to a structure.

physical hazards: Tangible risks like faulty electrical wiring, inferior building materials, or poorly constructed heating or air conditioning systems.

point of service plan (POS): A medical insurance plan that combines the features of an HMO and PPO. Within the network, the plan works as an HMO; outside the network, it has deductibles and copayments similar to a PPO. [See: HMO and PPO.]

policy: A written insurance contract.

policyholder: The owner of an insurance contract.

pre-existing condition: An ailment that occurred or was treated before a new insurance policy took effect.

preferred provider organization (PPO): A company that provides a network of hospitals and doctors for your medical coverage, but which allows you to go outside the network for a higher copayment. Deductibles apply.

premiums: Payments in return for insurance coverage.

proof of loss: Documentation submitted to the insurance company by a policyholder when filing a claim.

property damage liability insurance: A type of insurance that protects the policyholder from financial responsibility for damage to another person's property.

property insurance: A type of insurance that covers the policyholder for loss or damage to possessions.

protection amount: The amount of money that beneficiaries of a life insurance policy receive when the policyholder dies.

real property: A home and the land it is attached to.

recreational hazards: Risks posed by the leisure activities of individuals. Examples are racecar driving, bungee jumping, or sky diving.

renter's insurance: A type of insurance that protects policyholders who are tenants. Also Known as tenant's insurance.

replacement cost property insurance: A type of insurance that pays the policyholder the amount to replace items rather than paying the amount at which the items are valued.

rider: An addition to an insurance policy.

risk: The chance of loss. Insurance companies view an individual or the property insured—a car or house, for example—as risks, because that person or property could sustain a loss.

schedule: A list that itemizes insured property or possessions and the amount for which they are insured.

second party: Language in an insurance contract that refers to the insurance company.

stock company: An insurance company that is owned by stockholders or investors rather than policyholders.

tenant's insurance: [See: renter's insurance.]

term insurance: A type of life insurance that expires after a predefined number of years.

third party: An individual who seeks to be reimbursed by a liability insurance policy.

title insurance: A type of insurance that covers a land owner against liens on the property before title was granted.

total disability: An injury or illness that prevents an individual from working at any job for which the individual is trained.

umbrella liability: Coverage above the standard liability level.

underinsured motorist's coverage: A type of insurance that covers the driver and passengers of a car for losses if the at-fault driver has insufficient liability insurance.

underwriting: The process of selecting risks for insurance and determining the amount and the terms of the risk the insurance company will accept.

uninsured motorist's coverage: A type of insurance policy that pays the policyholder and passengers in the policyholder's car for losses caused by a hit-and-run accident or a driver who has no car insurance.

universal life: A type of life insurance that gives the policyholder the option to change the amount of premiums and death benefits.

vandalism: The deliberate destruction of property.

variable life insurance: A type of life insurance that pegs the death benefits and value of the policy to the rate of return on the investment of the premiums. Investments are selected by the policyholder.

whole life insurance: A type of life insurance that requires premium payments during the entire life of the policyholder and pays the beneficiary at the time of the policyholder's death. Whole life policies accrue cash value that can be used to make premium payments.

RESOURCES

Books

All You Need to Know Before Buying a Home. Wasfi Youssef, Ph.D. (Alpha Publishing, 1995).

The Beardstown Ladies' Common-Sense Investment Guide. The Beardstown Ladies' Investment Club with Leslie Whitaker (Hyperion, 1994).

The Beardstown Ladies' Stitch-in-Time Guide to Growing Your Nest Egg. The Beardstown Ladies' Investment Club with Robin Dellabough (Hyperion, 1996).

The Complete Book of Insurance: The Consumer's Guide to Insuring Your Life, Health, Property and Income. Ben G. Baldwin (Probus, 1996).

Market Driven Health Care: Who Wins, Who Loses in the Transformation of America's Largest Service Industry. Regina E. Herzlinger (Addison-Wesley Publishing, 1997).

Mercer Guide to Social Security. Dale R. Detlefs, Robert J. Myers, J. Robert Treaner (William Mercer, 1997).

Magazines, Newsletters, and Reports

Consumer Reports. (914) 378-2000, $24/yr. (Monthly except published twice in December).

Consumer's Digest. (847) 763-9200, $15.97/yr. (6 issues).

Consumers Guide to Long-Term Care Insurance. Elder Affairs, (800) 882-2003.

Outlook. United Service Life, (703) 875-3521 (semiannually).

You Magazine. Utica National Insurance Group, (800) 274-1914, $19.95/yr. (10 issues).

Appraisers

American Society of Appraisers. P.O. Box 17265, Washington, DC 20041, (800) 272-8258, http://www.appraisers.org

Appraisers Association of America. 386 Park Ave. South, Suite 2000, New York, NY 10016, (212) 889-5404.

Consumer Groups

American Association of Retired Persons. 601 E St., NW, Washington, DC 20049, (202) 434-2277, http://www.aarp.org

Consumer Federation of America. 1424 16th St., NW, Washington, DC 20036, (202) 387-6121.

Government Resources

National Association of Insurance Commissioners. 120 W. 12th St., Suite 100, Kansas City, MO 64105, (816) 842-3600, http://www.naic.org

National Flood Insurance Program, Federal Insurance Administration. 500 C St., SW, Washington, DC 20472, (800) 638-6620.

Property/Casualty Insurance, Insurance Information Institute. 110 William St., New York, NY 10038, (800) 331-9146.

Social Security Administration. (800) 772-1213, http://www.ssa.gov

Health and Life Insurance Resources

American Association of Health Plans. 1129 20th St., NW, Suite 600, Washington, DC 20036, (202) 778-3200, http://www.aahp.org

American Council of Life Insurance. 1001 Pennsylvania Ave., NW, Suite 500, Washington, DC 20004, (202) 624-2000, http://www.acli.com

The Council for Affordable Health Insurance. 112 S. West St., Suite 400, Alexandria, VA 22314, (703) 836-6200, http://www.cahi.com

Health Insurance Association of America. 555 13th St., NW, Suite 600 East, Washington, DC 20004, (202) 824-1600, http://www.hiaa.org

National Committee for Quality Assurance. NCQA Publications Center, P.O. Box 533, Annapolis Junction, MD 20701, (800) 839-6487, http://www.ncqa.org

Leading Writers of Property and Casualty Insurance

Aetna Life & Casualty Group. 151 Farmington Ave., Hartford, CT 06156, (800) 872-3862.

Allstate Insurance Group. Allstate Plaza, Northbrook, IL 60062, (847) 402-5000, http://www.allstate.com

American International Group. 70 Pine St. New York, NY 10270, (212) 770-7000, http://www.aig.com

CNA Insurance Group. CNA Plaza, 333 South Wabash Ave., Chicago, IL 60685, (312) 822-5000, http://www.cna.com

Farmers Insurance Group. 4680 Wilshire Blvd., Los Angeles, CA 90010, (213) 932-3200, http://www.farmersinsurance.com

GEICO. One GEICO Plaza, Washington, DC 20076, (800) 841-3000, http://www.GEICO.com

The Hartford Insurance Group. Hartford Plaza, Hartford, CT 06115, (860) 547-5000, http://www.thehartford.com

Liberty Mutual Group. 175 Berkeley St., Boston, MA 02117, (617) 357-9500, http://www.libertymutual.com

Nationwide Insurance Enterprise. One Nationwide Plaza, Columbus, OH 43215, (800) 882-2822, http://www.nationwide.com

State Farm Group. One State Farm Plaza, Bloomington, IL 61701, (309) 766-2311, http://www.statefarm.com

USAA. 9800 Fredricksburg Rd., San Antonio, TX 78288, (800) 531-8100.

Zurich American Insurance Group. 1400 American Ln., Schaumburg, IL 60196, (847) 605-6000, http://www.zurichamerican.com

Quote Services

InsuranceQuote, (800) 972-1104, http://www.iquote.com

MasterQuote, (800) 627-5433, http://www.masterquote.com

Quotesmith, (800) 556-9393, http://www.quotesmith.com

Selectquote, (800) 289-5807, http://www.selectquote.com

TermQuote, (800) 444-8376, http://www.rcinet.com/~termquote

Rating Service Companies

A. M. Best. Ambest Rd., Oldwick, NJ 08858, (908) 439-2200,
http://www.ambest.com

Duff & Phelps Credit Rating. 311 South Wacker Dr., Chicago, IL 60603, (312)
697-4600, Ratings Hotline (312) 368-3198, http://www.duffllc.com

Moody's Investor Service. 99 Church St., New York, NY 10007, (212) 553-0300,
http://www.moodys.com

Standard & Poor's. 25 Broadway, New York, NY 10004, (212) 208-8000,
http://www.ratings.com

Weiss Ratings. 4176 Burns Rd., Palm Beach Gardens, FL 33410, (800) 298-9222,
http://www.weissratings.com

State Insurance Departments

Arkansas (Rural), (501) 371-2640

California, (916) 481-1091

Connecticut, (203) 297-3902

Delaware, (302) 739-4251

District of Columbia,
     (202) 727-8000

Georgia, (404) 656-2056

Illinois, (217) 782-4515

Indiana, (317) 232-2385

Iowa, (515) 281-5705

Kansas, (913) 296-7801

Kentucky, (502) 564-6027

Louisiana, (504) 342-5423

Maryland, (410) 333-2521

Massachusetts, (617) 727-7189

Michigan, (517) 373-9273

Minnesota, (612) 296-6848

Mississippi, (601) 359-5969

Missouri, (573) 751-4126

New Jersey, (609) 292-6022

New Mexico, (505) 898-2356

New York, (212) 602-0359

North Carolina, (919) 733-2205

Ohio, (614) 644-2658

Oregon, (503) 947-7980

Pennsylvania, (717) 783-0442

Rhode Island, (401) 277-2223

Virginia, (804) 371-9694

Washington, (360) 753-7301

West Virginia, (304) 558-3354

Wisconsin, (608) 266-3585

INDEX